The Driller

Life Cycle

Bob Addy

Book Reality

Helping Writers Become Independent Authors

Cover Design by Brittany Wilson | Brittwilsonart.com

Cover Photo: by Keef Hickey | KeefPhoto.com Keef@KeefPhoto.com

Rear Cover: Professional World Championships, 1967 in Heerlien N.L.
Left to right: Gianni Motta, Ramon Saez, Jos Van der Vleuten, Bob Addy, Eddy Merckx.
Courtesy of Werner Möller.

I would like to dedicate this book to several people,
notably my long-suffering wife Wendy who has put up with me and my
passion for cycling and racing over fifty-five years.

My dear Mum and Dad who guided through my early years and Dad
whose encouragement, helped and pushed me beyond my wildest dreams.

My two sons Jason and Harvey along with their families,
and our two grandchildren Kate and Tom.
I hope they will find this a most interesting read.

Foreword

Where do I begin? I've heard people say Bob is a 'Marmite man', you either love him or you don't, which I can imagine is true but the point I'd like to add is, like Marmite, you'll never forget you've met Bob!

My fondest memories of working with him were my formative years as a junior cyclist. Bob managed the team I was part of in the Junior Tour of Wales. I was a first-year junior, but Bob's drive and ambition didn't have room for learning, we went there to win, and we did! It seemed so simple at the time as Bob did all the thinking for us.

As a rider he was fiercely competitive - and hearing from the people that have met him on the other side of the world - he still is! When he took the lead as a manger the competitiveness did not wane. To keep ahead of the rest Bob converted the training time as a rider to learning time as a manager, always seeking out – with insatiable appetite – the latest and most efficient methods of extracting performance. So much so, as I write this, I realise more and more how far ahead of his time Bob was. Many of the ways of thinking he taught me at the Junior Tour of Wales I still use today as Performance Director of a World Tour Team.

I was 2nd overall going into the last stage of that Welsh Race, over the mighty Tumble Mountain with the finish somewhere at the bottom on the other side. I can't remember exactly where the finish was, and that might seem strange as I was in contention for the win. The explanation: Bob! He made me focus on 'my finish line' which was the top of the mountain. 'Attack as hard as you can on the climb, forget what happens over the top, that will sort itself out' he said. A simple plan but sometimes they are the best and after all, it was a plan that worked. This was my introduction to what we refer to now as the 'phases of the race'. Our tactics are based on phases with each rider within the team responsible for a phase. This has been extrapolated to phase plans for all sorts now, rider seasons plans, nutrition and training but the idea is the same.

Some of his ideas weren't so glamorous though. On the split stage day, after the morning stage we were all sitting in a big hall with the rest of the riders waiting for the afternoon stage, chatting away. Bob came in after a few minutes and went completely crazy. Never stand when you can sit, never sit when you can lie down. We all duly lay down with our feet slightly in the air, much to the amusement of the rest of the riders in the room. We had a bigger smile later in the day though! Simple stuff but again the beginning of marginal gains.

I could go on all day about the lessons and ideas Bob gave me, some I can't shake even in everyday life. Nowadays, whenever I park my motorhome on an uneven surface, I always think of Bob. I must have my legs on the high end of the bed after he taught me to sleep at night with my legs elevated. In the end, Bob was ahead of his time. His insatiable appetite to learn was what he passed onto me, question the logic and continually move forward, because otherwise you are going backwards and the man we came to call, The Driller wouldn't be happy doing that!

Enjoy the book.

Roger Hammond

CHAPTER 1

WORLD PROFESSIONAL ROAD RACE CHAMPIONSHIP

I rode the hardest race of my cycling career in a town called, Heerlien, in the southeast of the Netherlands.

It was 1967 and after a very good season as a professional riding for Holdsworth Campagnolo in my first year with them, I was informed by the British Cycling Federation that I had been selected to ride for Great Britain in the Professional World Race.

Despite my limited program of road races, having to ride mainly criteriums in the U.K, I was soon pounding out the kilometres in training to prepare for the Worlds.

Not that I knew it then, but now, looking back, neither before nor after did I punish my body and mind beyond its limit to the extent that I did on that day.

The event was on a Sunday, slightly overcast, not a lot of wind.

The crowds were enormous, mainly coming from the host nation, but also from Belgium, Italy and France. My thoughts for the race were that I must try and get into an early break as my preparation had been so very limited. If that tactic was successful, at least I would get my name mentioned in the race commentary.

The top professional riders from the continent had ridden all the major tours and classics in their preparation, so they were seasoned, hard men. I had not had the same opportunities, so I was going into the event a little 'under done'.

***

I waited nervously on the start line until the bang of the gun went off. The ringing in my ears kicked the adrenaline in and we were away.

Immediately three riders attacked, Gianni Motta (Italy) winner of the

Giro and many top classics, Jon Van der Vleuten (Holland) a very good Pro rider and Ramon Saez (Spain) the Spanish Champion whose nickname was the 'Bull' and he was as strong as one.

My immediate thoughts were that I had missed the early break, but in the same instance, while I was still considering my options, the Belgian hero, Eddy Merckx attacked.

I could not afford to miss another opportunity, so I made my move, sprinting onto the rear wheel of Merckx, and we were away.

We both worked together for about ten kilometres to bridge the gap to the leading three riders. Once on to them, everyone was committed and going through hard lap after hard lap after hard lap.

I knew from past experiences that I had to keep eating and drinking, as this could be an awfully long day at the pace that was being set. I tried as often as I could to conserve energy, going to the back of the group to eat, missing the odd turn on the front, telling myself all the time to save energy.

Throughout, the crowds were going insane shouting for their favourite rider, Eddy being by far the most popular.

As the race went on, I could feel the constant speed was taking a toll on my body. The best thing I could do was to sit on the tail end for a while and pretend to eat. After doing this for about six kilometres, Merckx came back to me and said, "Englishman you go through."

I replied, "No, I'm knackered."

Within a couple of seconds, he was in front of me but he let the three others move away. The gap to them became bigger, maybe one hundred meters or more, then bang, he jumps across to them, a huge gap appears between his back wheel and my front wheel, slowly, oh so slowly, with every sinew straining, I staggered across the gap.

When I got back onto the four riders, Merckx turned to me and said, "You go through now."

And so, the torture continued.

The alternative would have been for him to do it yet again, so to avoid him isolating and detaching me, I went through then swung over as soon as I got on the front to save energy.

Oh, I must try to stay here longer… I might feel better soon. Here comes the hill again. Take my turn at the front, hope to still be with them at the top. We're spread across the road at the top of the hill with a three- minute advantage to the peloton.

I looked across at Merckx and he was having something to eat, at that moment I hate him.

The crowds are chanting his name "Ed-dy, Ed-dy."

The next time we go up the hill they are still shouting louder than ever "Ed-dy" but in my fatigued state, Ed-dy sounded like Ad-dy, Ad-dy, Ad-dy. That gave me a morale lift and I hung on a bit longer.

Unfortunately, two laps later, on the same climb, it would be the end of me. *Come on try, try, what is up with this body?* I keep sending down messages and five meters becomes ten meters and then fifteen, the gap is increasing to one hundred meters off the back of the group. Everything is so painful, my body is full of pain, then the crowd go silent, and I cannot hear a thing. I look across through glazed eyes, their mouths are still moving but why can't I hear anything. *Is this body of mine shutting down?* I get to the top of the hill and the break is out of sight.

I am told that Jan Jansen (Holland) is riding solo across to the break. When he gets to me, I tried to get on his wheel but it is not possible, it is as though he is on a motorbike, whoosh and he is gone.

I arrive back at the British pits, get dragged of my bike before the main bunch comes thundering by. They lay me on a bench completely drained and still aching all over. After some time, maybe fifteen to twenty minutes I sit up and slump forward, my body has had enough. Yes, I had eaten and drunk during the race, the preparation was as good as I could have managed without doing the big Tours and races beforehand.

I had given every last drop of energy and determination that I could muster for this World Road Race Championship. There was nothing more I could have left out there on the road that day, I'd given it my best.

Later on, Alex Taylor, who was the Manager for the day, informed me that the other team managers of the riders in the break told him to give me some mustard (dope) to keep me with the rest of the break. Alex knew my feelings on this from when I had ridden in the Tour de Avenir. No way, just coffee and a ton of determination was all I needed.

The breakaway stayed to the finish where Merckx won, Jansen was second, Saez third, Motto fourth and Van Vleuten fifth but he was later disqualified for taking too much mustard on the day.

Many years later I was in the Veterans six-day stage race in the Italian Dolomites. On the last stage Gianni Motta rode the first fifty kilometres as a guest rider. The crowds went berserk, shouting out his name "Gianni,

Gianni." I spoke with him as we rode along, and he remembered that World Road Championship in 1967 in Heerlien. He had trained by doing some three hundred kilometres non-stop for days on end. His coach told him, "You are going to be the strongest in the World Race in Heerlien. You have got to go from the gun."

Motta also said that when Jansen got across to them the pace went up another notch, so much so, that Eddy had to sit on the back for a while.

Later on, at the prize presentation at the end of the six day, I had won the over fifty-five age category despite being sixty-eight at the time and Motta, who was presenting the prizes, wanted to chat on with me much to the annoyance of the organizers who wanted him to present some of the other awards. It was just one example of old cycling comrades sharing their stories. And I have a lot to share.

CHAPTER 2

THE DRILLER - BOB ADDY

I arrived into the world half way through the Second World War, on the 24th January 1941.

Born in Luton, United Kingdom as Robert Charles Addy, I'd become better known as Bob Addy, or in the cycling world as, "The Driller."

My Mum, Frances, was born in Harlesden, north west London. Due to her mother having been married twice, my mother had three stepbrothers and two stepsisters. Mum had worked as a cashier in a Butcher shop in Harlesden before meeting my father.

Dad, George was born in Sheffield, Yorkshire. His Mum sadly died of the Spanish flu shortly after he was born. Dad had an extremely hard upbringing, so much so that at the age of sixteen he went to London intent on joining the Coldstream Guards, but was rejected for being underage, so six months later he tried again, and although still slightly underage, was accepted.

A few years later he met Mum, and they married in October of 1938. Shortly after they moved to a house in Luton where I was born. Eighteen months later my sister Susan arrived on the scene. Four years later my other sister, Wendy was born.

This last arrival was much to my disappointment; I had wanted a brother, so I would stubbornly nickname her "Bill" for many years.

Towards the end of the war we moved to live in Harlesden where the rest of Mum's family lived. This is where I started my first school, aged five in 1946. The Kebel Memorial School, later renamed, The John Kebel School.

When I was seven years old, I contracted measles which unfortunately caused me to go down with double pneumonia.

The doctor would come out to our house in the morning and evening every day for over two weeks as I was so ill. After a period of time I was sent away for six weeks to a convalescent home, thus missing over three months of schooling. My parents were advised by the specialist that because my lungs had been so badly scarred I should be encouraged to take up Sport.

That sounded ideal to me. Very quickly, I became well enough to become the captain of the school football, athlete and cricket teams. I was also selected to play football and run for the district sides teams. In athletics I was particularly good at sprinting and the long jump.

It was due to the encouragement I received through the school and the tremendous help from my parents that I recovered so well, so quickly. My lungs remain scarred to this day, but thankfully without any serious consequences.

Later, when I started concentrating on cycling, I would earn the nickname of, "The Driller." It came about due to training rides where I was always the one to keep pushing the pace up, hence people would say to me that I was trying to drill them out. It was reinforced in races, when in a breakaway, I would be the main instigator for increasing the pace and making sure that all the other riders were doing more than their fair share of work.

Once again people remarked that if you were to be in a break with The Driller, it usually stayed away and if you can't keep up, he will drill you out the back of the break.

I had started my cycling career from the entrance level of club rider and with good fortune and determination I ended up racing at the highest levels of my chosen sport. The Tour de France, World Championships, Commonwealth Games and Olympics. I rode against the best in the World in that era and would eventually complete the full circle, finishing up back at club level in Perth, Western Australia.

Many people have said to me, "it would be good if you put your cycling experiences down in a book." Most notably my good cycling friend, Brian Buck, who pushed me to make it happen. Never one to shy away from a challenge, I finally figured, why not!

CHAPTER 3

THE START OF MY CYCLING JOURNEY

The first bike I rode was a two-wheeler belonging to my sister Susan. A black, full-size wheel, no gears, ladies upright, which was brought for her by my parents for passing her eleven plus exams to go to the Grammar school in Kilburn, London. It had been hidden from her in Geoff Nash's garage where I worked in my school holidays from the age of eleven.

In 1953, the family moved from Harlesden to Ruislip, Middlesex and into a new semi-detached house. It was from there that Susan and I would take turns to ride and walk. One of us would ride the bike ahead, stop and put the bike in the hedge and carry-on walking. Meanwhile the other one would pick up the bike, cycle past the walker and do the same over again. This was our way of using Susan's bike and getting into the countryside.

When I was 12, Mum and Dad told me that the only way I would be getting a bike was to save up and buy one myself. After 18-months, I had saved up enough money from my paper round, garage work, birthdays and Christmas money to make my way down to Inward Cycles in Ruislip High Street. There in the window, was a blue Raleigh Lenton Sports with white plastic mudguards, four speed hub sturmey archer gears, drop handlebars and hub lighting on the front wheel. This at last was my bike. I was 14 and my pride and joy came at a cost of twenty-one pounds, fifteen shillings, (about £500 or $900 Aussie dollars in 2022).

On Sundays I would use my bike to explore the countryside. Eventually cycling as far as Oxford and back in a day, one hundred and thirty kilometres. I also started to use my bike to get to school and the Saturday job at the garage which was a forty-eight kilometre round trip.

At the age of 14, I thought up the idea that I would like to ride on my own to visit my Grandad who lived in Sheffield, a total of two hundred and sixty-eight kilometres in one day. This was to be done without the aid of a computer (which wasn't available obviously) but for some reason I decided not to use a map. I would be relying on my memory from when the family went by car to Grandads. I set off at four thirty in the morning and arrived at four in the afternoon, just under twelve hours for the journey.

One of my encounters on the way was with a couple of riders who had just finished a Time Trial on the Great North Road and they had their racing wheels attached to the hub of the front wheel. Little did I know at the time, just three years later, I also would be racing such events. I stayed with my Grandad for ten days and on one of those days I rode over to Manchester and back to see a cricket match at Old Trafford (one hundred and thirty kilometres) to which my Grandad said to me, "No, you have never done that.." So, I showed him my entry ticket to which he replied, "Bloody Hell lad, you have.."

Another day spent in Sheffield, I went with one of my uncles who had a maggot farm situated up on the moors. The land was owned by the Duke of Norfolk. It was comprised of a very big shed with square concrete bays, two meters by two meters by half a meter high. About twelve of them in all. Before getting there, we went to the abattoir to pick up some of the remains of the animals that could not be used. This was put into the bays which were heaving with maggots. My Uncle would put in a dye to change the colour of the maggots. From there he would sell them by the gallon tins to the fishing shops around Sheffield. The smell was horrendous. You could never get it out of your clothes no matter how many times they were washed.

The day had come for me to ride all the way back to London, again in one day. On my journey home, unbeknown to me, my dad and my Uncle Charlie came out on the Great North Road to meet me.

"You can get in the car." My Dad said.

"No, I've only got another eighty kilometres to go.." They could not believe it.

I must admit that later on, I had to stop to get something to eat, I was completely drained but eventually arrived home.

CHAPTER 4

1957 THE NATIONAL ROAD RACE CHAMPIONSHIP

The National Road Race Championship was to finish in Ickenham, Middlesex, some six kilometres from where we lived in Ruislip. The Club that promoted it was the Harrow and Rickmansworth Cycling Club. Dad came with me and we watched a thrilling sprint finish won by Stan Britain (The winner of the Tour of Sweden and many top-class races). He won from a group of six riders, one of which was Don Smith from Birmingham who we got chatting to after the event. He told us that he was selling another bike, the same as the one he had ridden in the race. The name was embossed on the top tube, *LeQuere*. It was hand built with light weight wheels and Campagnolo gears.

Dad turned to me and said, "Why don't you go and have a look at it."

So, the next stop was Birmingham with Don in his van, I stayed overnight and returned on the train with my new racing bike to which Dad said, "You had better join a Club now." And so I did. It was September 1957 and I was 16-years old.

During that winter Dad said, "You have to make your mind up whether you want to play football for Ruislip Town Football Club or take up Cycle Racing." I felt I was at a crossroads but it wasn't that difficult a decision for me. I opted to take up cycle racing as my primary sport.

The Harrow and Rickmansworth Cycle Club met on Monday evenings at a school in South Harrow. It took me three attempts before I plucked up the courage to venture in and I didn't bring my *LeQuere* in case they thought I was getting ahead of myself. Then again, each time the cyclists arrived I was worried my Raleigh Lenton would not be up to the machines they had. At last, I had the courage to go in one evening and got to know them (although I kept the *LeQuere* for my first proper race). They were a great crowd and greeted me warmly. I started to meet up on Sundays, go out on Club runs and also watch some of their Time Trials. It would be nothing to ride between 100 and 180 kilometres each Sunday.

One of the rides etched in my memory was when I met up with one of the rider's wife's whose husband was riding in a one hundred and sixty kilometre time trial. She was handing up food and a sponge to him at the event in Aylesbury, Buckinghamshire.

After the event, we started on our way back.

At one point this lady seemed to me to be going faster and faster. Turning to me, she said, "Are you okay?"

"Yes," I replied, "I'm alright."

"When did you last eat?"

"About six hours ago." This was my first experience of hunger knock.

She said, "I haven't got anything for you to eat."

So, for the next sixteen kilometres she pushed and encouraged me until she turned off. It would have been quicker if I had walked, I was going so slow. Once recovered, I could not wait for the next Sunday to be out with the club again.

The experience did not put me off, but I did remember it. As with all of those early rides, it was yet another lesson for me to take on board.

I rode most Sundays through the winter with the Club, but soon enough the day came round for me to enter my first race ever. It was March 1958 and I was 17. The race would start on the Watford Bypass, go through Berkhamstead, turn around almost in Tring, which was halfway, and then come back to complete the forty kilometre time trial. It would be the first day I would use the racing bike which I had bought from Don Smith.

The officials taped up the gears so that I could not use them above the restricted gear ratio allowance of seventy-two inches for all competitors.

Even now I recall the countdown as I was being held up by the pusher. Five, four, three, two, one and then I was gone. On my way, on my own for forty kilometres, going as hard as I could with my legs aching. I turned round near Tring where a Marshall stood in the middle of the road with a clip board recording that we had turned at that point. You also had to shout out your number when turning. On my ride back to the finish, I passed a few riders along the way. At the finish I was asked if I had turned round in the right place. I said that I had, but wondered why they were asking. Apparently my time, of one hour six minutes, fifty-nine seconds was only thirty seconds off beating the Club Champion at that time, Brian Parker.

"We will have to see if you went all the way round when the turn Marshall returns." The officials said.

A short while later the man from the turn at Tring confirmed that I had indeed got there. The rest of the season, my times kept coming down in the time trials events. I was making progress and the big aim was to try and beat one hour for the forty kilometres.

My racing to that point had mainly been time trials. However, at the firm I was working for as a trainee draughtsman, Acrow Engineering in Paddington, London, there was a lad called, Colin Spearman. He was the same age as me and had been competing in Junior Road Races (under-18s level). He convinced me to try my hand at junior road races.

The first race of my road racing career would an eighty kilometre event that finished on a hill near Amersham, Buckinghamshire.

I managed to stay with the main group until the final hill before the finish, but to my disappointment ultimately finished at the back of the field.

I started to enter several Junior events but was not always successful in getting into them because I had no previous results, and the field was restricted to the top 40 riders only.

The ones I did manage to ride in, I finished in the main group but found that my sprinting and climbing were not very good.

In fact, they were awful.

These weak links in my ability would be sorted that winter by Dad suggesting I do indoor fitness sessions which comprised of riding thirty-six kilometres to his school gymnasium (he was a Deputy Head Teacher) doing three laps of circuit training, getting showered and riding a further twelve kilometres into work. I would do this from Monday to Thursday.

Circuit training at the time had hardly been heard of and there were many remarks from fellow cyclists along the lines of, "You don't need that to go fast on the bike."

Dad was always ahead of everyone in his methods and ideas, some of which I still use to this day in my own coaching of riders.

On Monday and Wednesday evenings after work, I went to a weight gymnasium to do weights for an hour before riding home. Tuesdays and Thursdays Dad ran an evening class for cyclists of which there were around 20 of us doing circuit training again and general fitness. The modern-day terminology for all of this is, "Building up the core muscles" in your body.

All of this training meant I had just Fridays not going into a gym of any sorts but still had a forty-eight kilometre round trip into work and back on the bike. This would be followed at the weekends riding on Saturday and Sunday which would bring my total for the week to over eight hundred kilometres.

There were no trip-computers in those days, so the distances were worked out assuming we were travelling at twenty-four kilometres per hour average.

CHAPTER 5

CHANGE OF CYCLING CLUB

During the winter Dad and I thought it would be a good idea to change clubs and join the Ross Wheelers. One of the main reasons for this came from Dad's wisdom. If you go to another club which has got a higher standard of competitors, it will help raise yours accordingly. This rationale would also be applied later when entering races. In the Ross club the rider John Finch had finished runner up in the National Best All-rounder competition which was time trials over eighty kilometres, one hundred and sixty kilometres and 12 hours. With this in mind, I started to meet up with the club on Saturdays and Sundays during the winter at the meeting place on Richmond Bridge and we would end up riding between one hundred and eighty to two hundred and twenty kilometres.

By the time I arrived home I would be completely knackered.

One of the other club members was Mick Shea who was later to become one of the Country's top riders gaining selection for the Commonwealth Games in Jamaica and would ride in many international races on both track and road.

He became my brother-in-law, marrying my sister Susan.

Every year during the early season, one of the highlights was to ride the Bath Road Classic. A hilly eighty kilometres time trial which made its way along the river Thames near Reading to Wantage, Oxfordshire where it went up a hill. During the event the rider who started one minute behind me, Ken Kiping, a top rider of the day, had pulled back the deficit and by the forty-two kilometre point was alongside me. With a huge effort I managed to stay near him, occasionally overtaking him within the regulations until the finish which resulted in him being second and I was third.

Imagine my surprise when my photograph appeared in the weekly cycling magazine.

That result would be my passport into Road races which had been almost impossible before this time. Once again Dad would enter me in the best quality races in the area to improve my performances.

After many, many disappointments the results slowly started to improve. The races were generally between one hundred and twenty to one hundred and eighty kilometres at the weekends and the local midweek races were usually between seventy to eighty-five kilometres.

CHAPTER 6

TRAINING SCHEDULE

At the age of 18, I was working full time from 9am to 5pm at Acrow Engineers. My winter gym sessions would start at the beginning of October and go through to mid-February.

On Monday's the distance would be eighty kilometres, Tuesday one hundred and ten, Wednesdays, I'd managed to get the afternoons off, unpaid from work and do between one hundred and seventy to two hundred kilometres. Thursday one-twenty, Friday forty, Saturday, between one-forty and one-fifty kilometres and then Sunday, between two hundred and two-twenty, making for an average week of eight hundred kilometres plus.

All rides would be done non-stop and in the winter months the temperatures would be zero and below.

Some evenings I would start my ride from work in Paddington, and ride out forty kilometres, turn round, head back into the City where it was always a few degrees warmer and most importantly the roads were clear of ice or snow and then ride home forty kilometres.

At the weekends, a group of around ten riders would meet on a regular basis and do the longer rides. On occasion we would have to stop because we could not feel our feet with the bitterly cold, wet weather. This would be elevated to some degree by us running for about one kilometre to get the circulation back in them. Our hands also suffered from the extreme cold despite very heavy woollen gloves.

On many occasions, the drinks in our water bottles would start to freeze. To try and overcome this I managed to make up a thermos type bottle where I cut two drinking plastic bottles in half, put a thermos infill and insulating material in to line it so that it would keep the liquid warm for around about two hours.

The other hazard we had was early mornings when we had to be aware of the black ice on the roads. This initially would look as though it was just wet until you found yourself sliding on the road, making holes in your clothing and taking skin off.

Another element of the weather was when we had freezing fog and rain with icicles forming on our brake cables. Obviously, some days when we had snow this would cut down our kilometres, so once again we would ride into London where the roads had been cleared.

Our clothing would consist of a woollen hat or balaclava with layers of jumpers on the top, long john woolly underwear with corduroy trousers and long socks. Newspaper was also put up the front of the jumper to stop the cold air from penetrating through. If it rained, as it often did, you just got soaked and very cold. All the bikes on our training rides had to have mudguards and at night-time a good set of lights. If you arrived at one of the training rides without mudguards you would be told in no uncertain terms you would not be welcomed on the rides until you had some fitted or to sit on the back of the group.

During the winter there would be a number of reliability trials very similar to the modern-day charity rides. Generally these were held over distances varying from one hundred and sixty to two hundred and forty kilometres. To get to the start of some of these would mean an additional ride of between thirty to forty kilometres there and the same journey back home. These reliability trials would be run off at an average speed of between thirty-two to thirty-six kilometres per hour starting off with groups between twenty to twenty-five riders. The groups would gradually thin out as the kilometres and the pace took its toll.

We used heavy winter bikes and the ride was done non-stop, no waiting for anyone. At the end, back at headquarters, you were provided with a drink and piece of cake. Some of these events would be held on Saturdays and Sundays before the race season started at the beginning of March.

Most winters I would use a fixed wheel bike similar to a track bike up to mid-January then change over to a road bike with gears. The fixed wheel bike would perfect your pedalling action and also give you better control and balance in the ice and snow conditions. The gearing would be small, sixty-four to seventy inches, with two brakes and fitted out with the usual mudguards and lights. One of the main reasons for having a bike with a fixed wheel was that in the winter the road authorities would put down salt and grit to try to keep the roads clear. This would have a disastrous affect, corroding your equipment on the bike especially the alloy and steel parts. This meant a constant washing down of your bike after every ride.

CHAPTER 7

TOUR OF BRITAIN PREPARATION

In 1960, at the age of 19, my aim was to try to be selected for the following year's Southern Regional Team in the 14-day, Milk Marketing Board sponsored, Tour of Britain. It called for very hard training throughout the winter, with gym work thanks to Dad as well as working full time.

I hit on the idea of combining two weeks' holiday from one year's annual leave and the two weeks of 1961 together to have the month of February off. After much persuading the boss of Acrow Engineers, where I now worked as a fully-fledged draughtsman, granted me the leave.

The plan was to go to the South of France, notably Nice, and train in better weather and hopefully ride with some of the top professionals who train and race there every season. Then come back and get selected from good results in the early season races in the United Kingdom.

My journey to the South of France started on the 3rd February, 1961 when I boarded a train in London which took me to Dover for the ferry across to France. The crossing of the English Channel was very rough, so I was glad I didn't have anything to eat on the train beforehand. Arriving at Calais, I had a job to try and find the right carriage but after trying to explain in my schoolboy French, and with much waving of hands, I found the right one. The people sharing it with me were a man and his wife going to Nice and another woman going onto San Remo in Italy.

The couchette (bunk bed) was as comfortable as could be expected apart from the bumping and rocking of the train. Despite this I had a good sleep. The next morning, I woke up to a beautiful sunrise behind the snow-capped mountains. As the train made its way along the coastline you could see groups of riders training on their bikes with the blue Mediterranean Sea in the background. When the train arrived in Nice, amazingly only five minutes late, I immediately rushed out and went to the goods wagon at the back of the train but no bike was to be seen anywhere.

Once again a lot of explaining and hand waving, I was to understand that it would arrive possibly on the next train or one after that. With this information I gathered my bags and got a taxi with the other two people from my carriage who were going into Nice..

In the town itself, I wandered the back streets behind the promenade, a busy road with trolley buses going up and down on the wrong side of the road to my British mindset. In a short time I was lucky to find a bed and breakfast and midday meal. The landlady was to provide me with a breakfast which would contain fresh bread, marmalade and coffee. The room was on the ground floor and looked out onto a front garden full of palm trees. .

Later on, I walked back to the station to see if my bike had arrived and "yes, there it was". It had arrived on the second train. What a relief.

The next day, Tuesday the 6th of February, I got up at 7:30 in the morning, had my breakfast and then ventured out onto the front road. I was fortunate to see four professional riders coming the opposite way, so I turned round and joined on the back of them. We proceeded to go to Cannes where we turned right and headed inland to the hills.

I managed to keep up with them. On the ride I got talking to one of the professionals, Pierre Everaert who could speak good English. He was a roommate of Tommy Simpson and Brian Robinson on some of the tours. He also informed me that there were no races for amateurs in the area at this time of the year, which dampened my hopes.

After the training ride, which had lasted just over five and a half hours (one hundred and sixty-five kilometres), I'd had more than enough and went back to my accommodation for a wash down. I then took some fruit and chocolate to the beach where I lazed in the sun till about six in the evening, had a walk along the promenade then back to my digs feeling shattered. I had a good dinner at 7:00 that evening, was in bed at 7:45 and fell straight into a deep sleep.

The following morning did not start very well as the woman owner said she could not get up so early to prepare the breakfast (7:45). So, I opened one of the tins of corn beef that I had brought with me and a couple of bananas.

On meeting the four other riders we went in the opposite direction to the previous day, to Monaco, where we turned left towards the mountains, they were not hills.

The first went up a lot longer than the ones in the Lake District in the United Kingdom. Not as steep but about eighteen to twenty kilometres long. I managed to stay with them and got dropped by about thirty meters at the top of the first climb but caught them on the descent. The next climb I was completely drained of energy. I am not ashamed to say I was pushed up the last few kilometres by Rene Privat, a very well-known and respected professional rider.

The mountain we had just climbed had big banks of snow on the side of the road. At the top we all stopped to eat and drink. Privat gave me some of his food. It contained a cake with honey and sugar in it. Once I got back to Nice, I went out and bought two packets of it. Again, before we descended, we put paper underneath our jerseys to keep us warm. When we arrived at the bottom we could smell the rubber from the brake blocks. We then proceeded into Nice to arrive around 1:30 in the afternoon after five and a half hours.

One of the things I had to do after having my shower was take my bike to the local bike shop to have a peg re-brazed on which had come loose on the second mountain. It cost me the princely sum of fifteen shillings. I returned to the digs, polished off another tin of corn beef, some of the cake I had just purchased and a couple of bananas.

The next day, the Thursday, I intended to go over the border into Italy in search of some tyres. The professional riders were not going to be training and they advised me that you could get equipment a lot cheaper in Italy because they did the same thing when they wanted something special.

So it was that I went to Italy. On my way there, I encountered one of the professional teams, fifteen riders, all with green track suits and with their cars following with spare bikes and wheels. What a way to train!

I managed to find the shop just over the border. Apparently a lot of the riders went there. I was just getting my tyres, Campag Gear Rollers and a few hats when I heard someone say, "A Jack Hearne bike" in reference to the bike I was using at the time.

I turned round to see Ian Moore who had been staying in accommodation just outside Nice and paying two thousand and fifty francs to my one thousand five hundred.

Seemed the quality of accommodation and service was the same as mine, so my deal was a pretty good one. He had already been there about a month. He asked, "Who are you? I've seen your face before."

"Bob Addy."

"That's right, Ross Wheelers. I've read about you."

I ended up buying about eleven pounds' worth of equipment, six tyres the equivalent of one pound twelve shillings and sixpence each, which was half the price I would have paid in the UK.

Returning to France I caught up the following day with, what I now thought of as, my training group. There was Pierre Everaert, who had led for three days the Tour of Spain and finished fourth overall, been a winner of the Paris/Brussels and come second in the Liege-Bastonge-Liege. Pierre was a big domestic for the five-time winner of the Tour de France Jacque Anquetil.

Rene Privat, a solo winner of the Milan San Remo, winner of stages in the Tour de France and had also held the Yellow jersey.

Robert Cazala in the same team as Privat, again with stage wins in the Tour de France and finally, Albertus Geldermans, Liege-Bastonge-Liege winner, who would go on to finish fifth overall in the Tour de France, Yellow jersey for two days, Dutch road race Champion and stage wins in the Tour of Spain and a tenth overall finish in that Tour.

On my next ride I had with them, Privat was asking why I did not race, I told him I could not because I was an amateur. He explained that I should turn to become an independent which at the time was a class of rider who could ride against both amateurs and professionals. Pierre said that the place for me to go would be Brittany, but he would also have a word with both Simpson and Robinson tomorrow at the Grand Prix Monaco to see what they had to say. Pierre also said he would introduce me to the French riders, Anquetil, five times winner of the Tour de France and Anglade, one of the top riders in the professional peloton.

The day arrived of the Monaco race and I met up for the first time with Tom Simpson. Pierre had also been talking to Simpson and he had suggested that I turn independent as soon as possible and said to me, "remember it's not a sport, it's a business."

I charted the distances done every day, remembering that I had just turned 20 in the January beforehand. Most of these rides were done non-stop at around twenty-four/twenty-six kilometres per hour average.

Tuesday 6th February, 165 kilometres.
Wednesday 7th, 170 kms.
Thurs 8th, 125 kms.
Fri 9th, 190 kms.
Sat 10th, 165 kms.
Sun 11th, Rest Day.
Mon 12th, 130 kms.
Tues 13th, 220 kms.
Wed 14th, 95 kms.
Thurs 15th, 205 kms.
Fri 16th 165 kms.
Sat 17th, 150 kms.
Sun 18th, Rest Day.
Mon 19th 235 kms.
Tues 20th, 125 kms.
Wed 21st 130 kms.
Thurs 22nd,160 kms on my own for four hours fifty minutes.
Fri 23rd, Rest Day.
Sat 24th, 180 kms.
Sun 25th, 150 kms.
Mon 26th, 170 kms.
Tues 27th, 120 kms.
Wed 28th, Rest and travel home.

CHAPTER 8

TOUR OF BRITAIN SELECTION

After a lot of success racing in March, mainly due to my fitness from the training in the South of France with the professionals, I got notification to say that I had been selected for the forthcoming Tour of Britain (Milk Race) to ride for the Southern Regional Team.

The race was due to be held from the 4th – 17th of June, 1961, starting and finishing in Blackpool and racing over a total distance of two thousand four hundred kilometres.

The field would be made up of teams from Great Britain, Czechoslovakia, Denmark, Poland, Spain, Scotland, Wales, combined services of the British Army, Royal Navy and Royal Air Force and four regional teams from the North, South, East and Midland regions of England.

There were six riders in each team making a total of seventy-two riders in all.

My age at the start of the Tour would be 20 years and 4 months, which put me as one of the youngest in the race. The distances I had been doing in February in the South of France were a good platform and very good preparation, but I was still working fulltime 42-hours per week at Acrow Engineers.

My team officials on Southern Regional would consist of a manager and a mechanic who was only available for one week because that was all he could get off from work.

We did not have the pleasure of a masseur on our team.

The team comprised Warwick Dalton, a New Zealand rider riding in the UK at the time along with Keith Butler, John Clarey, Charlie Parks, Vic Mullaly and myself.

The distance of the stages in most cases would have an extra ten to fifteen kilometres to the official start, this was called the neutralized zone taking the race out of the towns to the start.

Stage one was from Blackpool to Nottingham, a total of two hundred and three kilometres. This was run off at an average speed of forty-two kilometres per hour. It was by no means a flat stage, it included an eleven kilometre climb at the one hundred and ten kilometre mark, named the Cat and Fiddle, then onto the moors at Cromford. (This area would become a happy hunting ground for me later in my career.)

Due to the race speed, the stage finished twenty-five minutes up on schedule.

I had managed to stay with the thirty-nine-rider lead group, with Pete Chisman winning in a solo ride off the front.

Stage two from Nottingham to Southend was to be the longest in the Tour, two hundred and forty-five kilometres on a very hot day which had us on the road for six hours and twenty-one minutes of racing. I finished in the main group but was absolutely shattered.

Alan Perkins won the stage. Warwick got across a three-minute gap and finished fourth. The peloton, which I was in, finished two and a half minutes behind.

I was so glad to see Dad at the finish at Southend and he was able to give my legs a decent massage.

As was the case at most of our accommodation, our bedroom was on the top floor of a Boarding House, four floors up and no lift. You had to take your cases up the stairs which was a struggle after having been on the bike for six hours.

My roommate was Vic, who had had a very bad crash that day and had been patched up by the race Nurse. Normally this would have been part of the masseur's roles. Seeing how bad he was, and we only had a double bed, I said, "You have the bed." I got the pillows and slept on the floor. So, after a two hundred- and forty-five kilometre stage, I did not have the best night's sleep.

Every night we had an evening meal in the accommodation, which was never enough, so we would have to go out and get another one in the town. In between all of this, we were responsible for checking over our bikes and on some days having to go with our washing to a laundry shop.

Stage three was from Sheerness to Hove, a total of one hundred and twenty kilometres which was to be a shorter but fast stage. Once again I managed to finish in the main field, only half a minute down on the leaders but still feeling the effects from the day before and the lack of sleep. The team was buoyed by the fact that the yellow jersey was on Warwick's shoulders. Albeit, only for a day.

Stage four was from Hove to Bournemouth, over one hundred and fifty-five kilometres. Unfortunately, after a substantial amount of hard work at the front of the Peloton, we lost the yellow jersey and Warwick would drop to third place at one minute and twenty-nine seconds behind the leader.

Stage five, Bournemouth to Cheltenham, one hundred and sixty-six kilometres was to be a very eventful day for us. John Clarey crossed the line third in the stage and Warwick had moved up a place to second overall. He also held the Points Jersey and John, because of his third place, was now second in the same competition.

I remember on the way into the finish with sixteen kilometres to go we had our first rain of the race. This was accompanied with very large hail stones, so big that all us riders finished with bruises on our arms and legs. Yet another day to try and find more food in the evening and to get our racing kit washed and dried.

Stage six, Cheltenham to Swansea, one hundred and ninety-three kilometres. This was going to be the first stage in the hills of Wales. The pace was easy enough for the first fifty kilometres before we hit the hills where there was a lot of splits in the Peloton and re grouping. John again finished with an excellent third place. Warwick was still second overall and still leading the Points. I finished in the same group as John.

Stage seven, Swansea to Aberystwyth, one hundred and twelve kilometres. Short, but brutal. Freezing rain all day. The first twenty kilometres were all uphill into the Black Mountains with moor land roads, very narrow with sheep wandering over them. The rain hammered down, onto an appropriate hill called the Devils Staircase, it was narrow with 1:4 and 1:3 gradients and was classed as a Premier Category climb. It was so steep in places the cars were boiling over and stalled.

I was zig-zagging up the climb when Bill Bradley, a previous two-time overall winner of the Tour of Britain, walked past me. "Save your legs Bob," which I did by getting off and walking with him. Down the other side of the hill taking many risks on the wet roads we regained the group. Warwick by this time had gone up the road in a break and was to finish third and once again take over the leader's jersey. This would mean some more hard work would be required by myself and the rest of the team to defend the jersey.

On this horrendous day, John would finish seventh, I came in twelfth and the rest of the race was splattered over the Welsh hills with riders coming in over the next two hours. The event in this era had no time limit for dropped riders, so they could roll in at any point and still be allowed to start the following day.

Stage eight, Aberystwyth to Buxton, two hundred and twenty-seven kilometres. The second longest stage of the tour and unbeknown to me at the time, was going to feature a very important location in my cycling career.

All the really hard climbs were to be in the last twenty kilometres. I managed to get away almost straight from the start in a group of thirteen riders. Keith Butler and I were there in defence of Warwick in the Leader's jersey and the main bunch unfortunately had gone to sleep and were not chasing hard. Keith and I were hoping to help Warwick over the climbs towards the end of this stage. By one hundred and fifteen kilometres we were informed that our group was now seven minutes in front of the yellow jersey.

As we climbed out of Congleton at two hundred kilometres Keith attacked, winning the hill prime and carrying on alone. The roads were greasy and wet racing into Buxton, with a few of the riders coming off on the descent. The break split into ones and twos and I would finish in seventh place, only one minute down on Keith the winner.

Unfortunately, Warwick had lost the jersey and was absolutely fuming about it. He was now fifth overall. I was seventh and Keith eleventh.

At last, we had good accommodation and we did not have to go out searching for food in the evening. This brutal stage had been run off at over forty-one kilometres an hour average.

Stage nine, Buxton to Skegness, one hundred and eighty-four kilometres, was to be the fastest average speed of all the stages in the Tour at over forty-four kilometres per hour.

Once again Keith was in the major break and finished third. After much work for Warwick, we did not lose any more time overall and he managed to finish seventh on the stage, John was tenth and I was in the middle of the same group and still holding onto seventh place overall.

Stage ten, Skegness to Scarborough, two hundred and twenty-one kilometres. Another very hard day with a strong head wind. The breakaway got away and we had all missed it this time.

Billy Holmes was the overall race leader with his team trying to limit his losses and once again Warwick had slipped down to seventh overall, I was now ninth, Keith in twelfth. The good thing was that Warwick still had the points jersey and John was still holding second in the same category.

Stage eleven, Scarborough, was a forty kilometre time trial.

After ten stages without a rest day, this was our virtual day off. It was not a flat time trial and had two hills that were 1:10 gradients. The weather provided us with extremely strong winds coming off the North Sea. Warwick showed everyone in the race how strong he was by winning on the day. Keith was twelfth and I managed fourteenth and slipped down to tenth overall.

Stage twelve, Scarborough to Whitley Bay, one hundred and seventy-one kilometres and once again we still had a horrible, strong headwind which kept the field together. John got into a late break and won the stage, which was a fantastic morale boost. Behind him the rest of us came in small groups and as a result of this I was now thirteenth overall. Warwick was fifth and Keith had moved up to eighth.

Stage thirteen, Whitley Bay to Morecambe, one hundred and ninety-two kilometres. One of the hilliest stages of the tour with major climbs every twenty-five kilometres with the peloton splitting and regrouping in between the climbs. I managed to stay in the front part of the race helping Warwick and once again battling high winds and pouring rain. Warwick and I finished in the main group. He retained fifth overall and still retained the Points jersey. Keith was eighth and I was still hanging in with thirteenth place overall.

Stage fourteen, the last stage from Morecambe to Blackpool, one hundred and ten kilometres short, but again with three very big climbs. No flat criterium as they have in the big tours now. Warwick was again very aggressive and made it into the break of the day with about eighty kilometres to go. He showed everyone how to sprint, winning the stage into Blackpool.

He had managed to climb back up to third overall and took out the points jersey award. Keith finished ninth and I was thirteenth. Our Southern Regional team ended up second overall in the team competition.

Wow what a race! I had lived my dream and wanted more, which was to come sooner than I thought. After the race finished on the Sunday it was back to work on the Monday having had two weeks off without pay.

CHAPTER 9

EARLY MONUMENT RACES

One month after the finish of the Tour of Britain on the 16th of July 1961, I rode in the Baz Wells Memorial road race promoted by the Actonia club.

The event was open to semi-professionals (independents and amateurs) for a total distance of one hundred and eighty kilometres over an extreme hilly course in the Chilterns.

The field consisted of riders from all over the UK, twenty-three semi-professionals and the rest amateurs. Some notable riders in the program including Barry Hoban who later won seven Tour de France stages. Hugh Porter, four times World Professional Pursuit Champion and a Tour de France rider. Warwick Dalton, third in the Tour of Britain, and nine other riders who had also ridden in the Tour de France.

The field was restricted to just fifty riders with eleven reserves. I was the eleventh reserve on the list even though I had finished thirteenth overall in the Tour of Britain. After waiting around, the organizers decided to let me start ten minutes before the off. It was a very, very fast start until we reached the three laps of a fifty kilometre circuit which included three of the hardest hills in the Chilterns: Chinnor, Kop and Kingston. Each of them having steep 1:4 gradients.

On the first lap a break of eight riders got away and I was still in the main group. At the end of the second lap with four big climbs to go I put in a very hard attack and got away, but had Doug Collins in tow with me, a very good independent rider who had a teammate in Alan Jacobs up in the break which by this stage was three minutes up the road.

I knew these roads so well from having done the majority of my training on them and now had some very good form from the Tour of Britain race as well. Fifty kilometres of very hard chasing saw me on the last climb,

Kingston, barely twenty seconds down on the break. I could just see them. Doug, who had been sat on for the majority of the way, came up alongside and said to me, "You go on Bob, I'm completely buggered trying to stay with you." With a huge last effort, I caught the remaining break just over the top of the climb. There were only four riders left, all semi-professionals. One of them called, "Where on earth have you come from?"

I replied that I had been chasing them for over fifty kilometres. At the finish there were five of us sprinting for the line and I managed to finish a close third. The rest of the field finished more than six minutes later.

This was another big step forward for me in one of the top class races in the United Kingdom.

Unbeknown to me at the time, my next race, a week later, was the Vaux Gold Tankard race which was regarded as second only to the National Road title in status. (Classified as a *Monument*.)

A field of the best riders in the country, with seventy riders entered, was run off in the Newcastle area over a total of two hundred kilometres. The winner was Bill Bradley (a former National Champion and also a two-time winner of the Milk Race). In second place was Billy Holmes who had just won the Tour of Britain and in third was Warwick Dalton who had finished third overall in the Tour of Britain. I managed to come in ninth place, much to my disappointment at the time as I felt really good during the race.

***

These two races, against the best in the UK, alongside my performance in the Tour of Britain made the selectors invite me to ride for the first time in a Great Britain jersey at the six-day Tour of Sweden stage race. The rest of the team was made up from Warwick Dalton, Ian Reid who had held a leader's yellow jersey in the Tour of Britain and was called back from France for the event. George Bennett who had won the King of the Mountains overall in the Tour of Britain and me. The manager was Bob Maitland a very experienced rider with wins in top class events, and the mechanic was my old mate, Jack Hearne who supplied me with my bike and equipment at cost price which was a tremendous help.

We travelled from Harwich to Copenhagen on an overnight ferry. Warwick, Jack and I were in the same cabin. I have never seen anybody as hairy as Jack and Warwick said to me, "We've got a bloody gorilla in with us Bob." Jack swung up into the top bunk cussing us as only Jack knew how to.

On the first stage the list of riders included Gustav Schur, Bernhard Eckstein, both from East Germany and former World Amateur Road Champions. A Belgian National Champion and also a Swedish Road Champion. In all there were ten teams of four riders.

The weather and road conditions were some of the worst I had encountered. Rain, wind, plus un-sealed roads, but the crowds were enormous, and the accommodation was fantastic. On stage one I was unfortunate that the down tube on my frame broke where it connects with the head tube with twenty-three kilometres to go to the finish. This left me with the wires from my handlebar controls holding the frame together. We had no spare bikes on the car that was following, which was just an ordinary salon provided by the race organization and had our mechanic, Jack Hearne, sitting in the back with some wheels. I lost nearly twelve minutes on what had remained of the front group. At the end of the stage Jack managed to get me another frame from the German team which he made up overnight.

On one of the later stages, again pouring with rain and a lot of dirt roads, I managed to get away in a nine rider group with Warwick, but unfortunately during the stage Warwick punctured his rear wheel. I waited at the back of the group for him to come into view so that I could drop off and tow him back on. The wait had seemed like an eternity. When he eventually caught up he was cussing and swearing about how Jack had got out of the car while it was still moving, shouting and swearing at the driver to stop, at which point Jack's foot went under the back wheel of the car but he still grimly held on to the bike wheel in his hand. When he got to Warwick, the rider had said, "Stop the monkeying about, Jack and get that bloody wheel onto my bike."

The scene must have been quite hilarious with Jack hopping about trying to get to Warwick to change the wheel.

Coming into the finish there were only six of us left in the group. I turned to Warwick and said, "I'll lead you out for the finish.". He had one of the best sprints around, but with one kilometre to go the Belgian rider in the break swung me wide and I found myself in the grit beside the road, immediately puncturing my front wheel. Despite that, I carried on to finish in sixth place with a flat tyre. Warwick finished in second place asking me, "Where the hell did you get to?"

We all had a good laugh about Jack and his antics and Warwick said, "I thought he was going to come swinging through the trees like a bloody big ape."

On the last day into Stockholm, the team manager Bob Maitland decided we would keep the race together, thus enabling Warwick to have a good chance of winning the stage. Warwick's reply was , "I'll show them how to sprint."

And wow did he, he won by three lengths easy.

I managed to finish 19th overall just one place behind Warwick, with George Bennett ninth, and Ian Reid thirty first. A real experience for my first ride in a Great Britain jersey.

One of my first races on returning to England, finished at the top of Ivanhoe Beacon. I won it and immediately after the finish Roy Thame of the Holdsworth shop in Putney came up to me and asked, "Where's your Jack Hearne bike?"

I explained about it breaking on the first stage of the Tour of Sweden.

"Would you be interested in riding one of my frames and I'll supply you with some equipment as well?"

I replied that I'd have to ask Jack, as he'd been so very good to me with my equipment previously. This I duly did and typical of Jack he said, "Go for it mate, go for it, he's got more f------- money than I have, and anyway, you'll always be known as one of the Jack Hearne boys."

He was right and it proved to be that way on many occasions throughout my racing career; a fact I was extremely grateful for.

When I retired from racing and opened up my first bike shop, Jack again would help by spraying the frames which Wendy took up to him and collected again.

Also, at that time there was a young lad who had been nicknamed Jaffa (Geoff Orange) who worked at Jack's. Jaffa would be a mechanic on the Tour of Britain in 1962, at only 16 years of age. Both Jack and Jaffa have been great friends ever since. Jack helped organise many races, also helping riders with equipment, including Eddy Atkins, a prolific time trial Champion and a former Hemel Hempstead rider.

Sadly and unfortunately, Jack died a few years ago.

CHAPTER 10

HEMEL HEMPSTEAD CYCLING CLUB

With Roy Thame now supplying me with my equipment from the start of 1962, he suggested that I might like to join his club, the Hemel Hempstead. It would mean joining up with Michael Shea and Jim Hinds, who at the time was a very good international, having won three stages in the Tour of Britain. All three of us would be riding Holdsworth Bikes supplied by Roy's shop in Putney.

This was to be the beginning of the most successful amateur team in the United Kingdom.

Roy also approached my Dad, and asked him if he would run the team as the manager, which he accepted.

During the winter months we would meet up on training weekends, but the UK winter, from November through to the beginning of March was also the time for social activities, so quite a few annual dinner/dances and prize presentations took place.

One of the traditions that occurred was "cross toasting" which was when you would make a loud bang on the table with your spoon and the place would suddenly go quiet.

The person would stand and announce he or she would like to take wine with another person in the room, accompanied by some witty or not so witty remarks, and in some cases to present them with a gift.

On one of these occasions it had been heard that the hard lads of the club had been complaining how it was so cold on the rides that even their willies got cold, hence a number of us were presented with colourful woollen willy warmers to which almost immediately a toast was raised.

How did the ladies know all their sizes?

With shrieks of laughter, the evening got more and more merrier as the wine flowed and the piss taking continued.

Later in the evening the prize presentations would take place and then a live band would follow.

One year we even had a number of dancing girls, who joined in much to the delight of the men folk at the time.

The following day, a Sunday, would be the traditional very hard training ride, and those suffering from hangovers would pay the price.

Most weekends up to Christmas we indulged in many parties of some type or other. One that springs to mind was a young couple in the club who had just got married the weekend previous. A couple of us decided when the party was in full swing, we would sneak up to their bedroom and nail a couple of smoked kippers underneath the middle of their bed.

I understand from reports it took at least two to three weeks before they found out where the horrendous smell was coming from.

All good fun was had on Club nights with various games and many a courtship started. As long as the girlfriends accepted that there would be another person in the relationship, the bike, and all the training and racing that came with it.

On a few occasions, after having raced on Saturday and Sundays, I would go to the cinema on a Saturday night and most times fall asleep only to be asked later if I had enjoyed the film.

"Oh yes." I'd reply, lying through my back teeth.

In 1964, Jim Hinds left the team and retired from racing. Our new recruit was to be Mick Brown whose previous club was The Edgware. He could be a fast finisher at times and would always give all that he had.

During this year we had twenty wins in the team on the road in some of the best races in the UK, with also some fifty-nine placings in the top six.

When riding in some of those races we would be up against the top semi-professional teams.

Dad, in his capacity as the manager had drawn up a contract for us mainly covering the prize money, behaviour, and press statements.

Often, we would be asked what races we would be doing in a couple of weeks' time so other teams could try to avoid competing against us.

The common remark was, "If you are going to be there, we don't fancy getting smashed again."

For Mick Shea this year proved to be a tremendous break through on the road. Myself, having come back overweight from Australia (more on that later), Mick had a ball torturing me no end on our training rides.

That year also saw the hardest winter on record. On occasions we had so much snow we had to use the car tracks to ride in with the wind and the snow punishing our frozen limbs. Makes me shiver to remember the pain he put me through. Mick was on fire that year, a force to be reckoned with, winning week after week.

He won the big classic early season event, the Archer Grand Prix, and also gained selection to ride in his first Tour of Britain.

I had a slower start to the year, yet by the end of it, I would be the British National Road Champion.

CHAPTER 11

SELECTION FOR THE COMMONWEALTH GAMES IN PERTH

The winter of late 1961 and the beginning of 1962 was spent training hard in the gym and on the road. I was working full time nine to five, Monday to Friday with Wednesday afternoons off without pay in preparation for the Berlin-Prague-Warsaw, fourteen-day stage race.

Two thousand, four hundred kilometres that would be run between the 2nd-14th of May '62. When I lined up for the start, I was 21 years of age.

Seventeen teams including one from Great Britain, consisting of six riders per team for a total of one hundred and two riders in the event.

On the first stage in East Berlin, we started in pouring rain, on wet cobbles over one hundred and thirty kilometres. At around sixty kilometres a huge crash occurred as the front of the peloton came down, Due to the weather conditions and trying to brake on wet cobbles, approximately fifty to sixty riders came off, me included. In all the confusion I didn't realise I had lost my watch in the crash, but unbelievably, some four days later, someone handed it into the race organizers who returned it to me with a broken strap. How lucky was I to have it returned?

One kilometre after the crash I found that I had punctured and had to wait at least four or five minutes for a spare wheel with the team car being held up because of the carnage behind. For the rest of stage I was chasing and finished some fifteen minutes down on the winners who had completed the race at an average speed of over forty-two kilometres per hour, some effort bearing in mind it was over wet cobbles in pouring rain.

Every day at the start of the stage the local scouts would present each rider with a neckerchief to symbolize friendship. A small token, bearing in mind this was at the height of the Cold War and East-West relations were not great. We then usually had between an eight to ten kilometres neutralized ride before the official start at the edge of the town. This part of the race was usually some of the fastest, as wherever you were positioned at the official start you tended to remain in an echelon position for the rest of the day. On a typical stage I would see a small village in the distance, and try to get across to the next group in front which could be the third or fourth group of riders on the road.

There was a sprint through these points of the race, with everybody trying to move up into the next group which at times may have been thirty to forty-five seconds in front.

As we approached the villages you could hear in the distance a brass band playing and we would hurtle through at over fifty kilometres per hour as the noise got louder and louder, after which we would come out of the village the same distance behind the group in front.

At the end of each stage we would finish on a cinder track in a stadium. As we stopped there would be a young lad with your number on a bib and he would bring your day bag with your tracksuit and towel in it. He'd escort you to a bus, put your bike onto a truck to be transported to the hotel and then by some means, he'd be waiting for you in the foyer, ready to take your case up to your room where the bike was already waiting, albeit still dirty from the day's efforts.

All the accommodation was the most luxurious I had come across. We all knew it was to impress us that life was good behind the Iron Curtain. The other thing that was impressive was how we had two team cars plus a spare third vehicle in case of one them broke down following the race.

After my disastrous first day, on the second day in East Germany, towards the end of the stage, I found myself to be the only British rider left in a peloton of thirty at the front. Our team car came alongside and told me to ease up and wait for our leading rider, Alan Jacobs, who on the previous day had finished in the main pack. We had some twenty kilometres to ride when he caught me up. I then towed him to the finish. As we entered the stadium a huge roar from the crowd went up, bearing in mind that at most finishes we had between sixty to eighty thousand spectators to watch us come in. I turned to Alan and said, "It feels as though we're winning the race and not finishing two minutes behind the leaders." I recall that as the main feature of the stages, the huge crowds and the very high speed.

It seemed as though every day we had cross winds, cobbles and pouring rain. I learnt more from this race than any other since I started racing, mainly on positioning and riding in echelons.

One of my lasting memories from Poland is finishing a stage to find two soccer teams, that had been playing in front of an eighty thousand crowd, had stopped their game because the race was finishing ahead of schedule. Imagine my surprise to discover one of the teams was Port Vale from England and they were cursing because the game had been cut short. I called out to one of the players, "Cycling more important than football, makes a change, mate!" He couldn't believe we were also from the UK.

Another thing that stood out in Poland was how the lads who greeted us at the stage finishes and escorted us, valued any food we offered them. I had been advised to bring fruit and chocolate as they were virtually unattainable in the country. When I gave the lad an orange, he thought that it was some kind of ball as he had never seen one before. I tried to explain by taking a segment of orange out of my back pocket and as he went out of the room he held the orange in the palm of his hand, gazing at it like it was a crystal ball. It was a very humbling moment. At the end of the almost two weeks of racing, I finished in forty-second position out of the eighty riders that completed the distance. However, that also meant I was only one second behind our leading rider Alan Jacobs.

**

My next race was the 1962 Tour of Britain, due to start on the 11th of June, allowing me some twenty-six days to recover from the eastern bloc tour. This Tour of Britain would be raced over two thousand, four hundred kilometres in fourteen days and I would be riding for the Great Britain team of seven riders.

In the first week I was going extremely well and on stage six from Bournemouth to Hove, a distance of one hundred and fifty kilometres, I achieved one of my goals.

Once the stage started, small groups eventually got together to form a leading peloton of twenty-two riders with all the big names in there. Everyone worked hard with nobody missing their turn on the front. We went up and down the small rises in the New Forrest with some switchbacks. Coloured jerseys bobbing up and down to the rise and fall of the terrain. Behind us in the main peloton there was panic as they realized they had been caught napping and were trying frantically to get their bunch working to pull the leaders back. Heavy traffic on the road made this nearly impossible, all they could do was pedal along and fume.

As they hammered down a hill into Romsey, Milanovic (Yugoslavian) took off on the wrong side of the road, belting on with his head down and crashed into an oncoming car coming the other way. He landed himself in hospital. Could have been worse, considering we did not wear helmets back then.

Meanwhile up front the twenty-two of us were not having it all our own way. We also had to fight our way through the traffic along Winchester Bypass to West Meon with the bunch now two and a half minutes behind us. Coming through Petersfield the lead had increased to four and a half minutes. At Midhurst, Bill Lievesley (Southern Regional Team) took a prime and Keith Butler (Great Britain) took the next one at Petworth. The group of twenty-two riders keep rolling along at a steady forty-two to forty-four kilometres per hour. We hammered through the lanes, not giving and not expecting any quarter.

No split came, although one or two weren't doing their fair share of the work. The pace was getting faster as we passed through Steyning, next was Old Shoreham. We screamed through there trying to cause another split in our group but to no avail. The lead was now six minutes. Coming into Wellington Road I attacked, skimming alongside a couple of the cars while those behind moved out. I was so close to them, but I knew this was going to be my chance and I took it with both hands.

I started sprinting like mad to try to gap the rest of the group. My teammates could see the possibility of me winning the stage. Metre by metre I stayed in front, through difficult roads and streets, not daring to look back for the fear of them being on my tail. At one kilometre to go there was still the danger of pedestrian crossings, bus stops, cars being parked, old ladies walking dogs, children playing ball on the promenade and other obstacles to negotiate. With the pain in my legs, which I was desperately trying to ignore, I hammered along until at the last turn into Grand Avenue. Cutting the corner to gain extra metres and unbeknown to me Jim Hinds was trying to cut the gap with Billy Holmes and Keith Butler and the whole pack close behind. I sensed victory and took the stage by one precious second from Jim Hinds with Holmes and Butler coming in to make it a first, third and fourth for the Great Britain Team.

A very proud moment, not only for myself but for my dad, who was the masseur for the Regional Southern Team and his rider, Jim Hinds finished second. Wow, what a day for us all to remember.

The second week of the race did not go as well as I was suffering from the effects of doing the two big stage races at my relatively young age. It had finally caught up with me.

Following the tour, I decided to go to Rouen in Normandy, France. One of the main reasons for this was that the current amateur World Champion, Jean Jordon and the professional five times winner of the Tour de France, Jacques Anquetil came from the town and as always my policy was to go and race where the best riders were.

On my arrival in Rouen, I stayed one night in a hotel then went to the local bike shop and joined the VC Rouen Club. As luck would have it, in the shop at the same time was the local Club Champion, Jean Claude Wullemin who said he would ask his mother if I could stay at their place. This subsequently transpired and their house was at the bottom of an embankment where the trains went from Rouen to Paris. It took me at least a week to get used to the continuous rail traffic thundering by day and night.

The good thing was that I became one of the family and they would take me out to all the good local French races. Jean Claude would eventually ride in the Olympics in the Team Time Trial, he later turned professional for the Jacques Anquetil Ford Team and would finish sixth overall in the Tour of Spain.

In one of the races I was in, there was just two of us left in the lead break, the amateur French Champion at the time and myself. The Club could not believe that I had kept attacking him. I finished second and they asked me, "Do you realize who you have been attacking?"

I replied, "Yes, another French rider," much to their amazement.

During my time with the French club, I was informed by the British Cycling Federation that if I went down to Salon in Italy for the World Amateur Road Race Championship, I would get a ride. So, the family took me down with their tents but when I arrived at the British Headquarters, I was informed that I would not get a ride. I was bitterly disappointed and disgusted by this, especially as none of the British team that rode finished, and the French riders were all at the front of the race, one being the French Champion who I had been attacking some two weeks prior.

There was a good deal of backlash over the whole affair, and one good thing came from it; I received notification that I had been selected to ride in the 1962 Commonwealth Games road race in Perth, Western Australia.

The course was going to be around Kings Park, one of the world's largest and most beautiful inner city parks. After getting the information on the contours of the race, once again Dad worked out a replica course for me to train on before departing for the Games.

As an amateur from Britain, one of the first things I had aimed for was to represent my country in the Commonwealth Games. With them being held in Western Australia it was going to be a huge honour but also a big adventure to go all the way to the other side of the world. I was so excited when I got notification about being selected, I don't think I slept for two to three days.

My big adventure to represent England in the Commonwealth Games started at Heathrow Airport. The most immediate difference when I finally got off the last leg of the flight was that I had left a wintery England, to arrive in a very summery Perth. I remember getting out of the plane and the heat just hit you. We went to the Games' village, near City Beach, to find our accommodation was a new house which slept eight of us in the English cycling team. There was a dining room/hall just down the road in the village with a man at the door who would wipe the swarm of flies off your back before you entered through the fly screen doors. There was also a laundry, photography shop and a small souvenir shop. One of the things that struck me was that there was a big 'temperature clock' and most mornings when we came back around nine in the morning the temperature was already registering in the early nineties (Fahrenheit, back then). We went training most days at five in the morning because any later and the weather was too hot. We later learned that it was the hottest summer on record at the time. Sometimes the track boys would come with us. We had a look at the Kings Park course which was going to be used for the road race, due to be held on the 1st December 1962.

The opening ceremony was on the 22nd of November. Having never been to a games before, it was interesting. We marched into the stadium in our team issue uniforms (which I still have and am quite proud to say, can still fit into 60 years later!) the roar from the crowds sent goose pimples across my body and my fellow teammates felt the same. It's something that you never, ever forget. An absolutely fantastic life experience.

While in the stadium a fly-past of Vulcan bombers came over, the roar of their engines felt as though the stadium itself was vibrating with the noise and you could smell the aviation fuel fumes as they disappeared into the distance.

As for my race, well it was a good and bad experience.

I was going one of the best. Come the morning of the race I had a very slight stomach problem. As the race went on, I managed to get into a group of eight riders away from the main peloton. Then disaster struck, I started to get severe stomach pain and had diarrhoea. I had noticed that in Europe some of the professionals had actually managed to go to the toilet while still on their bike. I thought, well I can't let the leaders go, so I went to the back of the group and 'performed' no fewer than three times. Needless to say, it was a mess all over me and the bike, but I was still with the leaders until I think about five laps to go when I pulled up and collapsed at the side of the road. The next thing I knew, I was in hospital, where they would tell me that Wes Mason, had won. He was one of my teammates that had been in the leading group I was in. I was thrilled for him but disappointed knowing I had been going one of the best in training.

But for an English rider to win in Australia was a great achievement. The fierce rivalry between the Aussies and us was always a factor and we had beaten them on their own patch. It would have been strange for me to think back then, that Perth was later to be my patch too.

Addy, and Vleuten trying to hold onto Merckx in the 1967 Professional
Road World Championships with the huge crowd shouting us on.

First Senior Road Race in Harrow and Rickmansworth club, a slow puncture
with 10 kms to go. The finish was near Ascot Race course. On the left
Ron Johnson, Bob and Tony Hull just before the start.

The finish of a club Time Trial, second 1 hour 3 mins 58 secs for the 40 kms. Held on the Watford Bypass 1958 in the U.K.

The Classic Bath Road Hilly 80 km Time trial. My first photograph to
appear in Cycling Weekly. Finished third.
A hard climb going up Wantage Hill, in Oxfordshire U.K.

Pierre EVERAERT

Professional rider Pierre Everaert signed photograph. What he wrote became true two years later when I won the National Road Race Championship being the youngest up until then aged 22 yrs.

Finished Team Time trial Tour of Sweden. Left to right Bob Addy,
George Bennet, Warwick Dalton and Ian Reid.
This was my first race riding for Great Britain.

Tour of Sweden breakaway. Bob Addy No. 9 with double toe straps and
Warwick Dalton on my wheel following.
Unmade roads for the majority of the stages.

Bob winning the Tour of Britain stage six finishing at Hove after breaking away to finish on his own before a huge crowd.

Dad (George Addy) on the left in white overalls at the prize presentation after the stage six win at Hove in Tour of Britain.

Bob winning the British National Road Race Championship 1963
in a sprint to the line.

ROY GREEN

talks to Bob Addy, seen above winning the recent national road championship. *Right :* man behind Bob (being congratulated by Charles Messenger) is really the man behind Bob—his father.

1963

1963 National jersey presentation with Dad in the background.
A very proud moment for us all.

Wedding photograph with an archway of wheels
(a tradition for many racing cyclists in Great Britain).
8th October 1966 at the Waterloo Road Mission, Uxbridge. Chas Messenger,
Alma Thame, Mick Shea (Best man), Mo and Bob Pither, Roy Thame.

National jersey with the London and National Championship trophies and many others. Photo taken in the back garden of Mum and Dads house, Bakers Wood, Denham, U.K.

Tokyo Olympic frame and jersey race numbers 38 for the Team time trial held in appalling conditions.

The finish in Paris of the last stage of the Tour de Avenir 1964 finishing in 7th place with a breakaway group containing many future Tour de France winners.

The first stage 1964 Tour de Avenir finish.
Very very hot, held in the South of France.
I had a cabbage leaf at the back of my neck to keep the sun off of me.

Tom Simpson looking on with Bob checking his wheels, the day before the
Amateur World Road Championship, won by Eddy Merckx. Bob finished in
the main group sprinting for second place. Another very wet day.

In honour of the British Olympic Team

The Prime Minister

requests the honour of the company of

Mr. R. C. Addy

at a Reception at 10, Downing Street, s.w.1

on Saturday 7th November, 1964 from 5.30 p.m. to 7.00 p.m.

An answer is requested to:
The Private Secretary,
10, Downing Street, s.w.1

An invitation from Harold Wilson (Prime Minister) to No. 10 Downing Street for the 1964 Olympic Games Team which had performed so well.

BRITAINS MOST SUCCESSFUL Road Racing Squad

Holdsworth Team Photograph.

The Manx Professional race with Bob Addy 3rd, Arthur Metcalfe 1st and Colin Lewis 2nd. The three of us later all rode for Great Britain in the Tour de France 1968.

Tour de France Team photograph of the Great Britain Team 1968.

HOLDSWORTH *Campagnolo*

The individual photograph taken on the Isle of Wight with Colin Lewis in the background.

CHAPTER 12

PERTH, WESTERN AUSTRALIA

Perth plays a major part in the history of our family. Starting with my wife Wendy's auntie who came to Perth as a seventeen-year-old in 1912. In 1948, Wendy's two brothers Richard (Dick) and James (Jim) Hawker also settled in Perth.

Jim originally came out to establish an Australian branch of the Martin Baker Aircraft Company. He had been working as a sales representative, selling ejection seats, but unfortunately the plan did not materialize.

Richard worked for the Ford Motor Company as a mechanic in Perth.

Both would settle in the city, marry and have families.

Wendy had first arrived in the same year I had, 1962. But where I was here for the Games, she , at the age of fifteen, had come shortly after her mother had passed away. Accompanied by her dad, they stayed with her brothers until, unfortunately, her dad passed away some two years after their arrival. Wendy returned to England where she had four sisters and worked at the Martin Baker Aircraft Company where some would say for her, unfortunately she met me while I was working as a draughtsman.

We married in 1966 and would come to Perth on numerous occasions with our two sons Jason and Harvey to visit Wendy's brothers and their families. Harvey, our youngest, came over to stay and trained on his bike in the summer and picked up a part time job at Glen Parker Cycles bike shop which was run at the time by Dennis Lightfoot and Hilton McMurdoh. When Dennis saw Harvey's bike which was one of my, *Bob Addy* frames, Dennis asked, "Who's Bob Addy?"

"That's my dad, " replied Harvey.

Dennis said, "No, really? Around Merseyside in the United Kingdom, if someone was on the front in a group going hard, the shout went up you're doing a Bob Addy." He didn't know it was a person, he just thought it was a saying at the time.

A few years later both our boys came to Perth to backpack around Australia and met up with two women who would turn out to be their future wives. Jason's wife to be Yvonne and Harvey's wife to be Rachel both originally from the United Kingdom were also backpacking.

On my trips over I would bring my bike out and, on a few occasions, competed in races organized by the Peel Club with Harvey also on the start line.

On one trip, Dennis Lightfoot very kindly loaned me a bike out of the shop thereby saving me bringing mine over on the plane, for which I was most grateful.

As the years progressed, Harvey, Rachel and their daughter Kate decided they would come to Perth to live.

Jason and Yvonne had arranged to be married in Sri Lanka, but plans had to be altered to Jamaica due to a tsunami that destroyed the coastline. They also had made up their minds to go and live in Perth permanently and asked us to come as well. We eventually arrived a few months before them in September, 2005. The big decision was made easier that both my parents had passed away, although both Wendy and I still had sisters back in the UK.

We settled in Mandurah, just south of Perth, having been here on numerous occasions visiting brother Jim and his wife Uta. The boys settled in Perth and opened their own flooring business called Riviera Flooring and continue to do extremely well in it.

To our immense joy Rachel and Harvey had Tom, our grandson in 2004, who has not taken up cycle racing as both our boys had chosen to do in their younger days. It had sometimes caused a bit of trouble for Harvey to be told, 'your dad did this and that in his racing'. Once when this was said Harvey replied, "I go quicker than him in sixteen kilometre time trials."

Tom on the other hand has excelled at golf, becoming a scratch player at the age of thirteen and at the age of sixteen was ranked number one in the under-18 age group for the whole of Australia. At 17, he finished runner up in the English Men's Golf Championship from a field of over two hundred. As I said to him, "You don't get any road traffic on a golf course, so it's safer than riding a bike."

On one of my many earlier trips to Perth, before we lived here, I came across Geoff (Chopper) Marshall riding along.

"How far you going mate?" he asked.

"Couple of hours."

"I'll come along with you."

And off we set. The speed went up and up.

"Have you done much riding or racing?" he asked.

"Just a bit," I replied.

Sometime later I contacted Geoff to say we were coming to Perth to live permanently, so we teamed up on a number of rides while still not letting him know what racing I had done before.

One day he asked me, "Why don't you have a go at racing?"

After chatting with Wendy about this, I decided to have a go. Bearing in mind, by this stage I was in my 60's and long 'retired' from the game. At the registration desk of my first race with the West Coast Masters, I met Mel Davis who had ridden in some of the races in the UK and had represented Wales in those 1962 Commonwealth Games in Perth.

"What are you doing out here?" he asked and then proceeded to tell everybody what standard of racing I had done. My cover had been blown.

One of my races with the club was the Criterium Championships around Rockingham (another suburb south of Perth). I got away very early with Wayne Lally who said, "It's too early mate, I'm not working."

I replied, "Okay, let me know when I should go away." So, we sat up and waited for the group. I immediately attacked again with Wayne and Colin Rossiter. At the end of the race, I was to win from Colin, with Wayne in third place. I overheard someone say to Colin, "Thought you would have won that easy with your good sprint."

Colin's reply was a classic, "Blimey mate, the bloke who beat me has ridden in the bloody Tour de France."

CHAPTER 13

BACK IN ENGLAND - NINETEEN SIXTY-THREE

Arriving back in England in January 1963 from the Perth Games, I was very much overweight having come back from Australia by boat. It took weeks and I'd eaten more than I'd exercised. I was going to have to find a job and start training in one of the hardest winters in over forty years. The snow was steeped in massive drifts across the country and the temperatures plummeted. It was one of the coldest winters on record and became known as 'The Big Freeze' For me, it was the start to what would become one of the most memorable years in my cycling career and would end with me becoming the National Road Race Champion of Great Britain.

I had super form leading up to the National that year, having won the West London Championship, the All-London Championship, Hemel Hempstead Grand Prix, which at the time was one of the leading races on the calendar. I also had a second and a fifth on stages in the Tour of Britain and many other minor placings.

Ten days before the National Amateur Road Championship of Great Britain, I had gone down with a very heavy cold which curtailed my preparation.

The National was run over one hundred and fifty kilometres around a very hilly course in Buxton, Derbyshire. I decided before the start that instead of being my usual aggressive self in the race, as I was still feeling the effects of the cold, I would start conservatively.

After only thirty kilometres I was under considerable pressure. We had been up a long climb and I was dropped from the main group in the company of Roy Hopkins and John Clarey.

On hammering down and taking many risks on the descent, we three managed to catch up the main group. I subsequently kept near the front of this leading group without doing too much work and during the race had a number of riders come up to me asking why I wasn't attacking in my usual way.

Getting towards the end I started to feel really good and come the final sprint, which was very awkward, I managed to find a small gap on the inside on the slight rise to the finish. With three hundred meters to go I started my sprint waiting and hoping that no one would come by. I reached the line a good length clear of John Clarey, who at the time was one of the best sprinters in the United Kingdom.

The look on Dad's face as I pulled to a stop was one I will never forget. All the hard work that we had both put in had come to fruition. I was now the National Champion at the age of twenty-two, only five years since I had started my racing journey. I was presented with the National Road Champion Jersey by Chas Messenger, organizer of the Milk Race who was also from my division of West London.

If 1963 had been good to me, 1964 was to be one of the turning points in my life, not only on the sporting field, being selected for the Tokyo Olympic Games, but also meeting my wife to be, Wendy; who remains the love of my life some fifty-five years later.

How did we come to meet all those years ago?

I had just returned from the Tour de Avenir stage race and was working in the Drawing Office at Martin Baker, the makers of ejection seats for fighter aircraft. The lads in the office informed me that a gorgeous blonde girl had started as a Secretary in the Sales Office. A few days passed then a nudge and a wink summoned me to the window to watch this beautiful girl crossing the yard outside. After a few choice words we settled back down to the job in hand.

Two days later one of the boys said, "You fancy going into Uxbridge at lunchtime?"

"No way, I always play cards." But all things changed when he said that the blonde girl was having a lift in as well.

"Oh yes, I'll be there." Lunchtime couldn't come too soon.

The car pulled up, my mate and his girlfriend in the front and two girls in the back seat. I got in and sat right next to the blonde girl whose was introduced as Wendy. We had a short journey of eight kilometres to Uxbridge during which time I was thinking, *wow this is a bit of alright. Shall I or not, yes, no, bugger it.*

"Would you like to come out with me?" I blurted out.

A short pause which to my youthful anxiety seemed like minutes.

"No thanks."

I get out of the car and crossed the road, looking in a shop window at nothing and thinking that I could have been back at the office playing cards. Then to my surprise and delight there was a tap on my shoulder and a voice said, "Yes okay then."

What a result! I was floating on air. Fantastic!

"I'll meet you tonight at Uxbridge train station and pick you up in a car." And that was it – our first date set. Needless to say, on my return to the office, uproar welcomed me and there was a lot of mickey taking including someone asking, "What about the other girl you are seeing?"

I considered for a moment and replied, "This one is something else."

I managed to borrow my dad's car, a bright yellow Ford Zephyr with a front bench seat and column control gears and we met that evening as arranged.

I drove as far as Wembley Stadium as I didn't want to take the car up into London as it was Dad's pride and joy. We made the rest of the journey on the train to Piccadilly and on to Simpsons Department store to pick up some of my uniform for the upcoming Olympic Games. To my dismay they were just closing, but after I had explained to the man on the door why I was there, he said, "Oh do come in Sir, Madam."

We left Simpsons with a suitcase bearing the Olympic rings and all my Olympic clothes.

I thought we might go to the cinema, but after joining a long queue waiting to go in, I thought all the standing around was not doing my legs any good, so I suggested we go and have a drink instead.

"Alright, that's fine," Wendy replied.

On entering the pub and sitting down I asked what she would like to drink. Later I'd discover that she'd never had a drink before, but she'd heard people say gin and orange, so that's what she asked for. Up at the bar I ordered a double gin and orange and a stout shandy for myself. Naughty boy!!! The next time we went out was for an evening dinner of Chicken Maryland at an Italian restaurant near where we would end up holding our Wedding Reception at, Denham Lodge, Uxbridge.

Seven days after our dinner I left for the Olympic Games and was away for five weeks, coming back to continue our courtship.

CHAPTER 14

TRAINING AND MISDEMENOURS

In training groups, I was always the designated leader both in United Kingdom and Australia. The cry would go up, "Where are we going and what are we doing Bob?"

The UK runs would always start on the 1st of January , non-stop, one hundred and twenty kilometres, with a group of about ten riders.

Saturdays would see us coasting it to Bognor and back, between one hundred and eighty to two hundred kilometres. We would only stop to fill up our bottles and have a pee.

Sundays would be the same kilometres, but inland.

January and February were always damp and freezing cold, some days would see snow.

On training weekends at Ivanhoe Youth Hostel we would arrive on a Friday night straight from work. Saturday morning, medium/fast one hundred and twenty kilometres. In the afternoon a very hard eighty kilometres going through and off. (Alternating turns of pace at the front of the group.) Saturday evening a chat about race tactics, events and training.

Sunday morning a very hard one hundred and ten/one hundred and thirty. This would end up at race speed if you were still there for the last one and a half hours.

The Sunday afternoon would be sixty kilometres at an easier pace before the drive home. All of this would be non-stop with a following car and three groups of twelve riders. One of the emphasis quotes was by John Clarey (Tour de France rider) to Geoff Cross, a very strong rider, hard as nails and always had on his head a cheese cutter hat and a bag swinging on his back with his feed in.

"Geoff, I don't mind you going so hard but for F's sake, take that hat off, you're doing my head in." Needless to say, Geoff did not say a word but just went harder, adding more pain to the rest of us.

Pete Wells, a Hemel Hempstead rider at the time, another hard man, a brilliant time trialist, a champion one hundred miler, nicknamed 'rigor mortice' and again a man who only knew one speed, forty-eight to fifty kilometre per hour. That still hurts just thinking about it.

Eddie Atkins, twenty-five, fifty-mile champion time trialist. Winner of many, events, a very good road man.

John Dowling again a brilliant time trialist and a road man. Competed in many tours. One of his claims to fame was that he did an exceptional time trial over sixteen kilometres on his road bike, no aero equipment and at the time became one of the first riders to go under twenty minutes.

Brian Tadman, the joker of the pack. Known as Tad or the Bald Eagle. A junior National Track Champion and also second in the Amateur Road Race Championship.

Steve Heffernan, Lincoln Road Race Classic winner plus third in the World Pursuit Championship. A top rider for a number of years.

Many other riders went on to become National Champions, one notably being Clive Pugh, a brilliant time trialist.

My brother-in-law, Mick Shea winner of many road races and a brilliant track rider, represented England at the Commonwealth Games in Jamaica on the road. He also won the early season Archer Grand Prix and a Monument, as well as racing in the Tour of Britain and Tour de Avenir.

One of the incidents that stand out from our Ivanhoe weekends was when we were just finishing one of our Sunday afternoon easy rides and a motorist decided to swerve in front of us, put his brakes on and almost had four of us off. Then he stopped his car, got out and wanted, in his words, "To show us youngsters a thing or two." Turns out he wanted to fight us. Step forward Tad, who put his bike down in the road and started laying into him. The driver's wife came out wanting the husband to back down, but no, he kept on saying, "I'll show these youngsters a thing or two."

After a couple of minutes, with a blooded nose, he decided he'd had enough, got in his car and drove off. We all rode back to the hostel to reminisce how the Bald Eagle (Brian Tadman) had done a couple of rounds with the motorist.

One of my most frightening episodes on a training ride was when a truck overtook me. In those days they did not go as fast as they go now, so we would use them as a bit of assistance to improve our speed work. On this particular day as a truck came by I got in behind and to my utter dismay discovered he was towing a trailer. The vehicle immediately moved into the kerb, but I couldn't move inside because of the high kerb, so I was left wondering if I should jump onto the tow bar and let my bike go underneath the trailer. After what seemed an eternity of about ten kilometres the truck slowed down at some traffic lights at Gerrards Cross and stopped. I managed to move away from the truck onto the pavement. Very shaken but with another lesson learnt: Make sure there is no trailer behind the truck!

One of our evening training rides took us from Ickenham, Beaconsfield, High Wycombe, Chequers, Great Missenden, Amersham Tatling End and back. A distance of one hundred and five kilometres. On leaving High Wycombe with eight riders in the group we were overtaken and cut up by a car which caused one of the riders to come off. Needless to say this was followed by sign language and a few abuses shouted at the car. As we got going again the car had stopped and a Policeman, in uniform, got out. He told us that we should be riding in single file, (we had been riding two abreast), to which Paddy Ryan said, "You can't do anything mate, you haven't got your bloody hat on and furthermore, let's have your Police number. We'll go down to your station and report you for dangerous driving."

The Policeman replied, "Okay lads, just be careful how you ride."

Paddy would comment later, "Well that put him in his place."

We then continued riding two abreast on our way up Hughenden Valley towards Chequers, as usual at near race speed.

Another training incident involved a truck driver and our boxing champion, the Bald Eagle (Tad). As we were approaching Red Hill in Buckinghamshire, a truck driver decided he did not like us riding two abreast and promptly cut in on Tad and myself, causing Tad to swerve and almost come off. At the top of the hill there was a traffic jam and the truck had stopped. Tad said, "We'll sort this bloke out." Having drawn alongside the driver's door, Tad started to give him a lot of verbal, then with no more ado the truck driver climbed out of his cab. He was HUGE! Almost blocking out the sunlight and he said to Tad, "So what you going to do about it sonny?"

I helpfully said to Tad, "I'll hold your bike."

Tad dismounted, with his hand pump gripped ready for the fight. In a flash the truck driver grabbed hold of Tad's pump and threw it into a field.

Tad said, "That's my best pump and it's got a campag adaptor end on it!"

"The only end you're going to get, mate, is the end of my fist," the driver said, advancing forward.

We decided to make a hasty retreat.

On our way back from the ride we retrieved the pump out of the field.

On another Sunday training ride, with eight riders, we were on the other side of Guildford going up a long hilly road and once again the principal actor was the Bald Eagle.

Tad had been dropped going through Guildford by about thirty seconds. When we approached some traffic lights the opinion was that we would get through them before they turned red as we didn't want Tad to get back on yet.

As we approached the lights, they did in fact turn red but we carried on, bearing in mind this was early Sunday morning with no cars about, or so we thought. Unfortunately, the car coming behind us was a Police car which stopped us a little further on and started to lecture us about going through red lights.

Tad caught up to us and riding past shouted, , "I would book them Officer, jumping red lights is against the law."

When we got going and caught the Bald Eagle, I said to the rest of the group, "We'll jump the bugger to make sure he doesn't get on."

We sprinted past him flat out.

Along the top of the ridge from the hill I insisted that we kept Tad chasing at 300 meters from us for at least the next sixteen kilometres. To our delight he ran out of energy and disappeared in the distance.

We did however relent after another twenty minutes for him to stagger back to our group. I said, "We've been waiting for you to catch us up, what took you so long?" I didn't realize he could swear so much. It was unrepeatable.

One of the unwritten rules of racing is that if you have not contributed to the breakaway, you do not contest a sprint of any sort. With this in mind, in a race in Surrey there was a break of five riders, at the back of the break was a semi-professional (independent) rider Tony Mills, who had not contributed to the efforts of the breakaway. With a hill sprint approaching I turned to Tony and emphasized that I did not think it would be appropriate for him to sprint, to which he said, "I will see."

At the commencement of the sprint he started to come past me. I got hold of his jersey, he got hold of mine, we ended up going over the sprint line tugging each other. After the line we both got off our bikes and started trading punches.

Unfortunately, the Chief Commissaire was in the car following us and we were told in no uncertain terms, "You are both disqualified and will be going before a disciplinary committee."

Some two weeks later Tony and myself were called to the meeting in a village hall to put our case forward and then had to stand outside. We could hear what they were discussing and to my horror, one of them said the amateur rider, Bob Addy, should be banned from ever riding again.

When we were called in my punishment was a six week ban from racing and Tony being a semi-professional was fined the equivalent of ten pounds (the average wage at the time was seven pounds per week). Even before our hearing both Tony and I had made up and were the best of mates on the road.

On most Wednesday afternoons a training group would leave our shop at Ickenham, Middlesex as we closed early.

An average of eight riders would turn up. On one particular Wednesday a new rider turned up with a tub roll and a very long pump sticking out of it, to which I remarked, "Who's the wally with the bloody pump?"

As usual the pace of the ride was good, if not quicker than racing and the distance would be some one hundred and twenty to one hundred and thirty-five kilometres. At around ninety-five kilometres the cry went out that the bloke with the pump is off the back, needless to say we just kept the pressure on.

The following week the rider who had been dropped did not turn out. On enquiring what had happened to him, I was told that apparently he had burst a blood vessel in his leg and thumbed a lift back to London on a truck.

It turned out he was a very good six-day rider and we subsequently found his name was Gary Wiggins. (The dad of Bradley, or Sir Bradley as he is now!) Another one bites the dust, he never came out again.

On one of the 1st of January rides, we had our usual number of riders, plus a rider from Merseyside who had recently moved down to the Reading area. He was a first category rider and very useful on the road. Having come up Stoken Church Hill at race speed, we went over the top and there was the usual four riders out of the twelve which had started plus our new recruit.

When I went back and enquired why he wasn't going through, his muffled reply was, "You must be joking, my body is in turmoil." Which caused shrieks of laughter.

Clive Pugh, was a bit worried, "Don't stuff him up too much because he's arranging my new mortgage."

Despite a number of attacks, he was still able to hang on. Clive did get his mortgage and the fellow would say to him, "Those lads are bloody nutters."

Clive replied, "That's Bob Addy for you."

***

Another misdemeanour occurred on one of our Wednesday rides. One of our regulars was Tony Gowland (TG), a top class rider on the track and road, and fiery by nature.

A bus had overtaken us out in the Oxfordshire countryside, passing so close that a couple of us had to escape onto the grass at the side of the road.

TG could not believe his luck when the bus stopped further up the road to pick up a fare. He sprinted like mad after him.

When the rest of us got there he had already parked his bike against the front of the bus and was exchanging a few choice words with the bus driver. The driver decided that his best retort was, "Get on your f'ing bike, sonny."

TG decided to put a couple of right punches through the open window.

The bus driver challenged him, "So you want to have a fight then?"

TG went around to the passenger door in the hope of climbing in and sorting him out.

Immediately the bus driver pressed the button for the doors to close leaving a very irate TG on the other side.

I said to one of the lads, "Quick get his bike away from the front of the bus, otherwise this nutter will drive over it." He rescued it just in time.

Most weekends I was asked where were we going on the training ride that day. My reply was usually, "We'll coast it." Which didn't mean taking it easy, it meant us going down to Bognor, along the coast and back for a distance of a minimum one hundred and eights kilometres. Always nonstop other than a refuel of ten minutes. On a particular occasion, on our way back, the big group had split into two bunches.

We had dropped the weaker riders by at least ten minutes so everybody in the leading group came to the opinion that we'd stop at the next café to refuel, there now being eight of us.

When a couple of us came out of the café we could see in the distance the second group of seven riders, pounding along. The cry went up, "Here they come." Steve Hefferman was in the process of buying a 2.5d (two and a half old pennies) Mars Bar and the woman said to him, "I don't have any change."

With one hand on the Mars Bar and the other hand on a ten-shilling note, Heff turned and said, "Sod it, I've got to have the Mars Bar." He left the note on the table, paying about fifty times the rate he needed to and thereby owning the most expensive Mars Bar in England, all for the fear of not getting in the group.

Heff was knackered that day which was unusual as he was one of the big engines in our group. He should have bought more Mars Bars, but I guess he couldn't have afforded them!

A number of riders started out on the training rides but only lasted one, maybe two, rides with us as they were always run off at a very good pace.

Pip Taylor was one of those.

On a very foggy Sunday morning, having done a coastal ride the day before, we set off inland going from the Target roundabout on the Western Avenue heading towards Cambridgeshire. Again, another non-stop epic was commenced.

After some two and a half to three hours the question came up, "Do you know where we are Bob?"

"Of course I do," I lied casually, while thinking that with all the fog, I hadn't got a clue.

Another hour and a half went by and with the fog lifting I started to recognize one or two landmarks.

Pip was definitely taking a bender along with the Bald Eagle who at Hatfield had to stop and was seen trying to make somebody open up a closed shop on a Sunday so he could get some food.

Needless to say, we just pressed on, having dispatched Pip as well.

Pip at the time was a very good track rider to whom I said, "I think you had better stick to the track."

He only came out once more.

CHAPTER 15

NINETEEN SIXTY-FOUR. TOKYO OLYMPIC YEAR

With 1964 being an Olympic year, Mick Shea (MS) , our recruit Mick Brown (MB) and myself had trained through the winter extremely hard. One of our first tests with the Hemel Hempstead team was going to be the Guinness Sponsored International four-day cycle race held over Easter in Bournemouth.

One of our main aims for the race was to try and get MB selection for the Southern Team in the Tour of Britain starting in June. To this end both MS and myself were going to look after him during the race. On the third stage of one hundred and thirty-five kilometres, after numerous attacks, the peloton came into Bournemouth for a bunch finish. MS and I led out MB, but at the finish Dave Bedwell, who had been nicely positioned to come off MS's wheel, won the stage. MB had lost the back wheel of MS on the dash to the line and only finished fifth. After a lot of discussion on how he had made a big mistake in not hanging onto MS's wheel we came to the final day of one hundred and forty-two kilometres, the team decided to try and help MB but if the situation arose, I was to try and go for a stage win.

On the last climb of the stage with twenty kilometres to go I attacked as hard as I could on the climb out of Poole and hammered over the top giving everything I had. Gradually, I extended my lead over the peloton into Bournemouth to such an extent that with the bonuses for first and MB coming in second, also taking bonuses, it gave me the overall race lead.

MB duly got selected to ride in the Tour of Britain, a fantastic result for all of us.

With the four-days finishing on Monday the 30th of March, the next event was the Red Rose Grand Prix, starting on the following Saturday.

A two-day event, over three stages, starting in Manchester and finishing in Buxton. The first day was one long stage of 140 kilometres. The second day was two stages.

At Easter every year the other major four-day race was the Merseyside.

It was usual that the top riders from both events met at this two day to see who was the top man. A mixture of semi-professionals and top amateurs would compete. The first day from Salford over the many hills to finish at Buxton Pavilion Gardens, a distance of one hundred and forty kilometres.

The first few hours of the race were frantic with a number of very fierce attacks until a break of three riders got away. Notably Mick Cowley, a top rider with Tour of Britain stage wins, accompanied by the well-known, Bill Bradley, a twice National Road Champion and winner overall of two Tour of Britain's.

With a gap of one minute and ten seconds to the leaders and with forty kilometres to go, I attacked out of the peloton on a hill as the breakaway disappeared from view.

Some eight kilometres later I was on them and immediately went straight into a hard attack, dropping the other rider and leaving Mick and Bill to chase me. Coming down to the finish the three of us were going to sprint it out. The finish had a tricky, narrow entrance some two hundred meters from the line, first through it would win.

Elbows out, we hurtled towards the gap, Bill and I side by side, I got through for the win by barely half a wheel.

After the finish Bill turned to me and gave me a very big compliment, "How on earth did you manage to come across on your own when we were working flat out and out of sight of the peloton?"

***

Buxton in early April is very rarely a warm place.

On the morning of the second stage, I woke up to find the bed had a sprinkling of snow on it which had come through a slightly open window.

Luckily for the race the snow had cleared for the start at 9:45 for eighty-two kilometres of racing.

With continuous attacks trying to dislodge me and with the help of my team mates I managed to finish the stage safely in the yellow jersey.

One and a half hours later we started the last stage of sixty-five kilometres over an extremely hilly course. I was very pleased to see a group of riders go away that were well down on classification.

Derek Harrison narrowly won the stage from Albert Hitchen with the rest of us coming in some forty-five seconds down on them. At the end of it all I had won the battle of the South versus North all from my first day break with Bill Bradley and Mick Cowley. Another great weekend of very hard racing.

During my stay in Buxton, in the same accommodation was Pete Matthews from Liverpool who became a National Road Race Champion. He was also a bit like our Bald Eagle, always up for a laugh. He also became one of the very best wheel builders in the United Kingdom.

This was also the year I came second in the Manx International Road Race. An event run over three laps of the T.T. course in the Isle of Man.

The previous year I rode it, Doug Collins, a well-known and experienced international, advised me, "You can only go up that mountain flat out once, try and make it the last time."

With that knowledge in 1963, I was unfortunate to puncture on the first lap and had to go flat out on the second time up the mountain to regain the peloton and finished in thirtieth, well and truly stuffed.

Riding for the England A-Team in '64, we were against teams from the Continent and with one lap to go, Roger Swerts of Belgium had attacked and got away going through the grandstand straight. With some eight kilometres from the start of the mountain I attacked as did Les West, who was also in the England A-Team. As we were almost catching Swerts, I said to Les, "We'll go in the opposite gutter, and I'll attack him hard."

Bearing in mind the roads round the TT course were closed to traffic, I attacked as hard as I could, but he still had enough fire in his legs to reel me in with Les. Halfway up the climb Les put in a hard attack which meant I was to sit on until I thought I could cross over to him leaving Swerts behind. At that moment Eddy Soens came alongside on a motorbike and said, "You have got to sit on him."

By this time Les was some fifteen seconds up the road.

Coming down the other side of the mountain Derek Harrison (also England A-Team) had descended like a rocket and caught us up.

At the finish I jumped with three hundred and fifty meters to go, finishing second, some twenty-six seconds behind Les. Swerts was in third and Derek Harrison fourth.

The England A-Team won the team prize with first, second and fourth places. This was one of the performances that was to help me gain selection for the Olympics in Tokyo.

On learning I had been selected to go to the Olympics, my last event, some ten days before going to Tokyo, would be the Cherry Blossom One Hundred (named for the miles it ran over, it was one hundred and sixty kilometres in total), from Bath to Chiswick in London. The event attracted all the top riders throughout the United Kingdom as the first prize was one hundred pounds. A staggering amount given that the average wage was about ten pounds per week.

The race distance of one hundred and sixty kilometres was helped with a very strong tail wind. The attacks were fast and furious until a group formed of some eleven riders. The most notable being Dave Bedwell, Alan Jacobs, Albert Hitchen and myself, along with a number of top amateurs of the day.

On this day Hitchen was definitely on his motorbike, so much so every time he went through to do his turn at the front we were all in top gear trying to hang on with one and two lengths between the wheels.

He was doing five hundred meters on the front shouting at everyone to go faster. I was on my limit to hold a wheel as was everyone else. We eventually were stopped by the gates coming down at a level crossing. Albert did no more than shoulder his bike, run up the steps, over the bridge and down the other side. Dave Bedwell said, "Let the bleep, bleep go, he is tearing our legs off."

Can you imagine about six kilometres from the finish there was Albert coming back as though he had been shot.

We swept onto the cinder track at Chiswick, Alan Jacobs beating me to the line. For me the big bonus of second place was that I was the first amateur and I received prizemoney of seventy pounds to take away to the Tokyo Olympics, in tandem with some very good form as well.

Before going out to the Tour de Avenir, I rode in a series of races in East Germany. The team was made up of Hugh Porter (H), John Clarey (JC), Harry Williamson and myself.

The races were mainly criteriums plus a team time trial. In the criteriums,

JC was up in the front for the sprint finishes. In the team time trial H and I thought it would be great to hammer JC mainly because he was well known as a super sprinter who sat in most of the races.

In the sixty kilometre team time trial Harry was soon off the back of us, so H and I had a great time handing out a lot of pain to JC who eventually had to sit on. As we approached the finish H said to JC, "Now let's see you sprint."

There was no sprint from JC, just a few choice words.

After the finish he turned to us and said, "You have both ruined my legs forever." Walking away as though he had been on a horse for a number of hours.

CHAPTER 16

TOUR DE AVENIR

I decided not to ride in the 1964 Tour of Britain having ridden the previous three years and opted instead to ride in the Tour de Avenir.

It was a fourteen-day stage race for National Amateur Teams from all over Europe.

The route was to take in the last two weeks of that year's Tour de France in the mountains and the stages were run in conjunction with the Tour de France. On some days we would do the complete stage but start an hour before the Tour or sometimes thirty kilometres into their stage.

This would be the first time I had raced up the biggest climbs in France. On the first stage the temperatures were around 42°C in the shade and there was not a lot of it. It was so hot, the tar was melting on the roads as we set off. One of the things I did to combat the sun was to put a large cabbage leaf under my cotton hat so that it shielded my neck from the burning heat.

Being the current British National Road Champion, a lot was expected of me from the Press and the European National Managers. The winner of the first stage was Felice Gimondi, I came in with the main pack two minutes down.

Many of the riders from the teams had to pull out on the second day. In the Great Britain team, both Keith Butler and Ken Nuttall pulled out with sun stroke. This left us with five riders in the race.

As the race went on, I felt stronger and stronger and managed over the course of the fourteen days to have six places in the top ten, plus a third into Bordeaux.

On one particular stage that finished up the Puy de Dome, a non-active volcano, I encountered an Italian rider on the arduous final climb to the finish. Two riders were away and what remained of the chasing group of twelve riders were in the echelon. With the wind coming across our right shoulder and as I came down towards the back of the group, I felt a hand on my hip trying to move me over so the rider behind me could get more shelter in the echelon. After this had happened a few more times as we worked our way up the mountain, I lashed out at his arm. This had the effect of stopping him doing it and later on in the following stages we came to be the best of mates, letting each other into the line.

This rider was Felice Gimondi, who had won the first stage and would later win the race on the last day into Paris.

I remember on one stage, when descending down a mountain in the leading breakaway with all the top riders, on an extremely sharp bend I lost control of my bike and slid out with a thundering crash. My arm and leg took a shredding as I hit the road.

The bike slid on and disappeared over the edge, down into a ravine. So, there I stood, at the side of the road while my breakaway companions disappeared down the mountain. Our team car was way back behind groups of riders because the peloton had exploded up the climb. After a few minutes, to my good fortune, teammate Mick Shea came into view. He slammed on his anchors, stopping just a few meters away and in an instance, I was on his bike which was almost a replica of mine. Sometime later in the stage the team car drew alongside. They had retrieved my damaged bike by looping together tyres to hook round the bars and thus haul it out of the ravine. I stopped, got on my repaired machine and rode off, while they waited until Mick came along on a team spare bike and got back onto his own.

At the finish of that stage, I was most disappointed as the break I had been with finished five minutes in front of the peloton which I came in with.

On the very last stage into Paris, I was on fire. A group of twelve riders had broken away and had a lead of just over two minutes when I decided I would bridge the gap on my own. After a huge effort over ten kilometres I managed to get on the back of the group. Only one other rider got across that gap and that was Gimondi who got on a short while after me. His effort would enable him to win the Tour de Avenir overall. At the finish I came in seventh place with the breakaway consisting of top class riders who subsequently went on to win stages in the Tour de France. In the case of Gimondi and the French rider Lucien Aimar, they both won the Tour de France in the next two years and also many classics along the way.

My final placing was twentieth overall despite losing considerable time on a couple of the stages.

In Paris, our team manager Alec Taylor was approached by three different professional team managers from the Tour de France to see if I would be interested in turning professional with them. One of the main reasons they approached me was that during the Avenir race the team masseurs from all the countries would be bused from the start of the stage to the finish, awaiting our arrival. As they waited they had struck up conversations. One such had gone along the lines of, "What is your rider Bob Addy using in the stages because our riders are taking this and that."

Our masseur replied, "He doesn't take anything other than strong coffee."

"That's not possible as he has got up with the leaders on most of the days."

This was reported back to the professional teams who had also just finished their tour in Paris and their thinking was, how good would this rider go with the same things that we were supplying to our riders?

The conclusion to all of this was me telling Alec Taylor I would not be interested as I would not know what they were trying to put into me.

It was after the Tour de Avenir I was informed that I had been selected to ride the World Amateur Road Race Championships in Sallanches, France in which a young Eddy Merckx got away from the field on the last lap and won. I managed to finish in the main field sprinting for second place which was won by Eddy Planckart who did not realize his teammate had already finished.

In our team was Peter Gordon, who had won our National Road Race Championship, but did not start the race as the evening before he went by car with his dad to look at the St. Bernard Pass. After getting delayed on the way back he arrived at our hotel in the early hours of race day.

Chas Messenger, the manager of the Great Britain Team, had no compunctions about banning him from the start of the race even though he was our National Champion.

The following day in the World Professional Road Race, Tom Simpson put in a huge effort and chased the lead break for a number of laps on his own before eventually getting to them.

Mum and Dad had come over to watch me in the race and had slept in my car (a Triumph Herald Station Wagon). One of the British women's who was staying at the same hotel as us got chatting to Dad and asked for a loan of some money. She never did pay it back, much to Dad's disgust, him being from Yorkshire as was the rider.

CHAPTER 17

TOKYO OLYMPICS - 1964

I had been selected to ride in the road squad for the 1964, Tokyo Olympics. The rest of the team comprised Colin Lewis, Mike Cowley, Terry West and Derek Harrison. Chas Messenger would be looking after the road team and the overall manager was Tommy Godwin who would also look after the track team.

After the long flight to Tokyo, we settled down to some good training. I had some great form and was selected to ride in the one-hundred kilometre team time trial. Chas Messenger had left Terry West out as he felt he was not going as good as the rest of us.

I asked Tommy Godwin what was the chance of me riding in the road race as well, his reply was, "You are lucky to get a ride in the team time trial."

Well, that's all I needed to be told!

The day of the race was my type of weather, raining.

Our team was to start one place in front of the Russians who were one of the favourites to win the event. I said to the rest of the riders, "When they catch up, (which was inevitable), if we stick with them, we will be up there with a chance of a medal." Also, in the back of my mind was that this might be my one and only chance to represent Great Britain in an Olympic race.

What the Team manager had told me added more fuel to the fire for the race.

After about forty to forty-five kilometres the Russians were on us.

Let's keep with them, we must.

A short while after, Derek had gone off the back on a small rise as we were picking up the pace.

Mike and Colin said "We'll wait for him."

Bugger there goes our medal chances up the road.

Not long after, Derek drops off again, but this time we leave him. With some fifteen kilometres to go Mike is suffering and as the event requires three to finish, he sits on while Colin and myself are doing huge turns at the front. I keep thinking to myself, this is my last event and I push harder and harder.

I could not believe it when with five kilometres to go, Colin said, "You do the longer turns to the finish." which I did.

The rest of the team wanted to know if I had taken anything as I had been so strong.

Despite our efforts we couldn't keep in the medals, finishing at the end in 15th.

The team selected for the road race was Terry West, Colin Lewis, Mike Cowley and Derek Harrison. Chas Messenger who had followed us in our time trial had put my name forward to ride in it but, "No," came back the answer from the overall team manager, Tommy Godwin.

Derek at the time was riding a Tommy Godwin bike which demonstrated extreme bias to me and my form. The only official explanation was that Derek was an extremely talented rider, but at the time was not on his best form.

The finish of the road race was a straight road, slightly down hill, tree lined. The lads had asked, "What gears should we use for the sprint?"

Fifty-two times thirteen was my advice. (Fifty-two tooth front chainwheel with a thirteen rear cog.) My advice was based on having sprinted and done well against the majority of the riders there in the Tour de Avenir.

Derek said, "I only ever use fifty-one times fourteen maximum."

After the finish he said to me, "I wish I had a bigger gear at the end."

I walked away in utter disgust.

Some of the Olympic road riders from other countries asked me why I had not ridden in the road race as I had done well against them in the Avenir. I had no answer for them.

After all the road events had finished, we let our hair down a bit and went sightseeing. I shinned up a pole and got a flag (still have it). On one occasion we took some water pistols with us and went to a strip show and surprise, surprise we were asked to leave.

Another incident was when we were told that Saki is better heated up so one of us decided to put some in a kettle on the stove and warm it up a bit. Then a few minutes later someone shouted, "I think that the alcohol is warm enough, there's blue flames coming out the spout!"

On the plane coming back from Tokyo to Heathrow we were all informed that as Great Britain had performed so well in the Games (finishing 10th in the medal table) we had all been invited by Her Majesty the Queen to go to Buckingham Palace where she would be there to greet us.

On landing, I briefly saw my Dad and Grandad who had come down from Sheffield, but had to inform them I was required to go to a hotel and prepare to go to Buckingham Palace.

On the team's arrival our names were announced, and we were duly introduced to members of the Royal Family and were offered some light refreshments.

Wow, what an honour.

Another invitation was to visit the Prime Minister, Harold Wilson at the official residence, 10 Downing Street. On entering through the big black door, which was opened by a footman, I walked straight in and continued walking but was summoned back by one of the officials to shake hands with the Prime Minister, who I thought was the doorman.

I hadn't voted for him and anyway, I'd have recognised him better if he had worn his raincoat and carried his trademark pipe.

Another function I attended was the Lord Mayor's Ball in London. I took my new girlfriend, Wendy along as my partner. We met up with Huge (H) Porter (cyclist) and Anita Longsborough (swimmer) who would later marry each other, having met on the plane going out to the Tokyo Games.

Many other Club dinner/dances followed where I was the 'Guest of Honour' with Wendy as my escort, no doubt wondering who on earth this man Bob Addy was.

During the 1964 winter, Dad and myself decided I would leave the amateur ranks and become an independent rider, joining the most successful team, "Falcon" for the 1965 season. I was 24.

CHAPTER 18

THE START OF TRACK RACING

The first time I ever rode on a cycle track was in Perth, Western Australia. Karl Barton, who was the sprinter in our England Commonwealth Games Team, on most days, would come out with us for at least sixty kilometres before turning back to do track work in the afternoon. It was on one of these rides he suggested to me to come down to the track where we could borrow Harry Jackson's bike, him being the same build as myself and who was one of our team pursuiters.

When we went to the Lake Monger velodrome and I looked down from the top of the steep banking for the first time, I said to Karl, "Okay, I'll follow you, but only if you keep down the bottom of the track." That was the deal.

After a number of laps, he started to edge up higher and higher on the banking and eventually we were zooming up and down. I loved it, what a fantastic sensation.

Returning to the United Kingdom in '63, I had exchanged my air ticket for a boat ticket and arrived home nearly five weeks later. I was fat and unfit having put on some fifteen kilos in weight. One of the first things I did was to purchase a track bike ready for the track racing at the Herne Hill Stadium.

Every week throughout the summer my racing schedule would be road races of varying distances from one hundred and ten to one hundred and thirty kilometres most Saturdays and Sundays. Track racing was on Mondays at Herne Hill. Tuesdays were long rides to a total of one hundred and twenty kilometres and Wednesdays was back on the track at Herne Hill.

If there were no track meetings, I would ride Stoke Poges evening road races. Thursday evenings would be a sixteen kilometre time trial or a long training ride of over one hundred and thirty kilometres.

On Wednesdays at Herne Hill track there was usually a Madison event held on the program. I would team up with Mick Shea who was also in the Hemel club and was an extremely good track rider. Big and powerful with a good sprint. He was also a brilliant roadman.

As a team we became unbeatable. One of our strategies was on the first change of partners we would not change with the rest of the field but attack thus causing chaos with the riders missing their incoming partners. Safety-wise, it was also a good move. We would eventually always get a lap up and win with Mick getting most of the sprints, so much so that at one meeting we were told by Eddie Wingrave, "You are going to have a lap handicap because you keep winning."

We still won by gaining a lap back and then proceeded to lap them a second time.

All this track racing helped me to improve my sprint and speed and Dad reminded me, bearing in mind he had been onto me for at least two years to do this, that he was right again.

Later, I raced at the Wembley Indoor Arena where there was a competition for the riders who had not been selected for the six-day race. The series was run prior to the six-day riders coming out onto the track. I managed to win a couple of these. One in particular was the "devil take the hindmost" in which I took off and lapped the field.

I also finished third in the British Professional Pursuit Championships and had numerous wins and placings at track events.

In 1968, I started teaching at Herne Hill Cycle track five days a week. I was employed by the Inner London Education Authority where pupils (up to forty at a time) would be bused to the track as part of their sports morning, replaced by another group in the afternoon.

The other teachers there were Mike Armstrong, Bill Dodd's, John Clarey and me. My journey to the track and back on my bike accounted for a total of four hundred kilometres a week.

Six of the pupils who attended became top Amateur Road/Track riders, the outstanding one being Maurice (Mo) Burton, a Junior National Track Champion who competed as a professional in fifty-six, six-day races all over the World.

Much later, at a Cycle Trade Show in Birmingham as I approached the entrance, Mo saw me in the distance and came running over. He hugged me, then introduced me to his wife before telling her, " "This is Bob Addy. The man who made me the bike rider I was to become."

"Oh, I have heard so much about you from Mo," she said.

I was at Herne Hill Track for nearly four years from 1968, then spent 1972 with John Austin at Paddington Track, four days a week with pupils going through their paces there. Later, I would compete in the evening meetings there and then ride home to Hyde Heath, Buckinghamshire a total of fifty-two kilometres.

CHAPTER 19

FALCON TEAM AS AN INDEPENDENT

The year after the Tokyo Olympics Dad and I decided I would leave the amateur ranks after the disappointment of not riding in the Olympic Road race. The best Independent Team in the UK at the time was, Falcon Cycles. Albert Hitchen, a prolific winner at the time would be calling the tune on most of the races.

One early season race that stands out in my mind, was the Skelmersdale two-day race.

With around fifty kilometres to go on day one, Peter Buckley, a talented amateur, attacked up the road. I tried to get across to him on my own with Albert also making a solo attempt but neither of us could bridge the gap. Afterwards, in the changing rooms, I got a roasting from Albert. Standing in front of everybody he said, "If you are going across a gap, make sure you can get there, don't stop halfway!"

On the second day Albert decided he would attack with some forty kilometres to go. Then with eight kilometres to the finish we caught him in an awful state, unable to hang onto our group. After the finish I said to him, "What goes around, comes around." Sweet revenge for his sarcasm the day before.

***

The Tour of the Southwest was a top class classic seven-day stage race.

In the Falcon team was Albert, Bernie Burns a prolific sprinter and winner of many races. Billy Holmes, Tour of Britain winner, Bill Bradley National Champion, Tour of Britain winner and myself.

Bernie won the first three stages.

On the fourth day he came into breakfast having been up all night with a nosebleed. Bearing in mind that Bernie had the Yellow jersey, Bill Bradley said, "He'll be stuffed and not on good form. We'll have to look at an alternative plan."

On one of the following days, I managed to get into a break with just two of us left. Just before the finish I attacked to win on my own.

When Albert came in his remark was, "Good ride. And what did you take to win?" I told him in no uncertain terms my coffee as usual, nothing else.

"Well, I am telling you now, the peloton was chasing at full speed behind."

On the following day Bill Bradley said to me, "Look Bob, when I attack, you come with me and we'll stay away to the finish. You could be in second place overall and I will be leading."

Right on cue when Bill attacked, I followed him, and bingo, we achieved the results he had predicted.

At the end of the tour the Falcon Team came away with stage wins, and first and second places overall. We won over two hundred and fifty pounds each, plus our bonuses from Falcon.

Later in the year, I rode in the Tour de Avenir with the Great Britain team again. Despite being a marked man from the other nations, because of the previous year's result, I still managed a third on one of the stages.

At the British Independent Championship which Albert won, I managed sixth place. In this race I had again been away on my own towards the finish when Albert caught up with me and went by like a train.

At the end of 1965, the British Cycle Federation, along with the UCI decided that all independent riders could do one of two things. Either revert to amateur status or race as professionals.

My decision was to become a professional rider in 1966.

I took out a professional license without a sponsor and decided the place to go for the training and races would be to return to the South of France.

I travelled down with George Drewell, another professional, travelling down to Nice in my car and staying with Alec Taylor's mother who lived down there.

George and I managed to do a few training rides before the season began. One race in particular, was the biggest field I had ridden in, close on three hundred and thirty-five riders would be on the start line. Most notables being, Jacque Anquetil and Raymond Poulidor along with all the top professionals of that era. The race was one hundred and fifty kilometres.

You could hardly move up, down or sideways until Poulidor thought it would be funny to scrap his shoe with the metal plate along the ground to give the sound effects of a crash happening. Everybody suddenly found room to move, cursing him for a number of kilometres with me sitting comfortably behind Anquetil's wheel.

You could always tell if you were near Anquetil from the smell of expensive cologne which drifted back and his hair was always immaculate, in fact he always had a comb in his back pocket.

One of my best results in these races was a twelfth place in Frejus from a field of two hundred and fifteen riders. It was pouring down with rain and Vin Denson won on that occasion.

I did six races around Nice before motoring up to Ghent in Belgium, some eight hundred and fifty kilometres through France, in a day.

On arriving in Ghent I was fortunate to meet up with Keith Butler who was living there and he suggested I stay with him and his wife Marilyn.

My first race in Belgium was going to be the Ghent Road Championships over one hundred and twelve kilometres. Most of the English and Australian riders who lived in Ghent rode in the race. Most notably were Vin Denson, Alan Ramsbottom, Barry Hoban and Keith Butler.

As the race progressed, I found myself in a five-man break which included Vin. In the sprint to the line, Vin led out Benoni Beheyt, an ex-world professional road champion. I had just about managed to get on his wheel and finished second with Vin in fifth place.

After this ride I was asked to join the Leroux-Terrot Team along with Keith.

There were not many races in March, so I would go out training with the English and Australian riders including Tom Simpson who was the then World Road Race Champion and just getting over a broken leg he'd managed to do whilst skiing.

He said, "Bob, you need to give it a bit more than one hundred per cent in these races."

"Tom, I'm giving it one hundred and five now!"

Talking later to Vin he would comment, "That is Tom for you, one hundred per cent plus all the time."

The old question came up about doping. Vin suggested, "It was only taken for the Classics, The Worlds and the Tour de France."

"Not for me, thank you." I said.

Through my result in the first race, I was selected to ride for the Team in the early season classic, Het Volk.

After about one hundred and twenty kilometres of gutter grovelling, the group turned off the main road onto a very narrow cobbled road. The riders in front of me immediately took to the dirt at the side of the cobbled road where it was smoother.

"Bugger." I'd misjudged it.

I came off, hitting a metal angled post, jumped up, bike okay, and started chasing to get back on. A team car came up beside me and the manager yelled out, "I think you had better stop, your right shin bone is poking out of the skin."

Looking down with blood pouring out of it and the white bone showing through, I decided to pull out.

I went back to the café, changed, then to Keith's place. Scrubbed the injury out and bandaged it up, hoping for the best.

Seven days later, I was racing again.

At Easter, Wendy came over bringing some more wheels and equipment to replace some of mine that had been damaged by the Belgium roads.

Later in the year I went back to the UK to ride the Classic Tour of the Southwest, a seven-day stage race and I would compete in a composite team. During one of the stages that went into Paignton, I was away in a break which included Arthur Metcalfe and Brian Sandy. Both asked me for help to do most of the hard efforts at the front of the break for them to keep us away.

Arthur went on to win the stage and it put Brian well up in the overall classification. This result, plus being fourth on the stage was worth a good sum of money as both riders were very generous in paying for my services.

The race finished in Weston-super-Mare.

Wendy had come down with my parents to see the finish of the race and it was here I decided to ask her if she fancied getting married. We set a date for our wedding of the 8th October which was also my parents anniversary.

Wendy said that she wanted to go back to the continent in 1967 and would work when I would be racing, but I had to be honest in my answer.

"No, I know how good I am. I've seen enough of how some of the riders get their results, and it's not for me."

CHAPTER 20

1967 - START OF THE HOLDWORTH/CAMPAGNOLO TEAM

Without a sponsor for the coming season and with most of the teams in the UK being full, I approached Roy Thame of the Holdsworth Shop in Putney.

He was a member of Hemel Hempstead, the same club as me.

We came to an agreement that he would sponsor me for the season and incorporated the same colours as the Hemel Club, orange and blue. In mid-season, Roger Newton would also become a team member.

I had wins in the Brian Robinson Grand Prix beating Arthur Metcalfe in a bunch finish and would later win the Newcastle Grand Prix Road race.

It was also the year that I was selected to ride the Tour de France which, for the first time in a number of years, to be made up of National Teams as opposed to Trade Teams.

In preparation for the Tour de France, the majority of the team was racing in Belgium.

In one particular race of two hundred and thirty kilometres I got away with a Belgium rider barely ten kilometres from the start. With the two of us sharing the workload and prizes on the way, after one hundred and twenty-five kilometres I dropped the other rider. I was finally caught after having been out the front of the race for nearly one hundred and eighty-five kilometres and was immediately spat out the back of the main group, completely spent. I pulled out of the race.

Later, the team manager for the Tour, Alec Taylor, came to me and said, "You should still be out there racing."

In my shattered state my reply was somewhat to the point and subsequently I was taken off the team for the Tour.

The Belgium rider had also abandoned the race sometime before I had.

Looking back, in some respects it turned out to be a blessing as Tom Simpson, the leader of our team, died on that Tour and his death was a terrible blow to everyone who had ridden with him that year.

In 1968, one of the two notable races on the professional calendar in the UK was the Manx Premier Trophy race, preceded by the Classic Vaux Grand Prix a few days earlier.

Still riding virtually on my own in the Holdsworth colours, and having finished seventh in the Classic Vaux, I had extremely good form.

The Manx race was on an eight-and-a-half kilometre circuit.

I attacked with four laps to go from the finish, away on my own from the main peloton in an epic lone attack to the resounding cheers from the crowds who were being urged on by the commentator through the grand-stand section of the course on each lap.

Despite repeated efforts by the main peloton to reel me in I was only to be caught some five hundred meters from the line by two notable riders in Arthur Metcalfe and the then National Professional Champion, Colin Lewis.

Immediately, Arthur turned to me and said, "Come on Bob, keep doing a turn at the front."

The main group was now only three hundred meters behind us, chasing hard. Once again, I told Arthur to pee off. I had been away for what to me seemed an eternity.

Come the sprint Arthur won from Colin with me a close third.

That evening we had the official awards presented for the Cycling Isle of Man week and to my delight on being called up for my third position, I received the biggest ovation due to my attacking during the race.

In the same year I had two overall wins in stage races, The Cotswold two-day and the three-day Tour of the Hopfields. This was to help me get my selection for the fifty-fifth edition of the Tour de France with a total distance to be covered of four thousand, six hundred and sixty-five kilo-metres. (In the present-day tour, the latest one to be ridden as I write is 2021, the riders covered a distance of three thousand, four hundred kilo-metres.)

This was the Tour de France.

My boyhood dreams were to become a reality on the 21st of June 1968, starting in Vittel.

There would be one hundred and ten starters, eleven teams of ten riders and it would be the last Tour run with the National Team format.

One of my teammates was John Clarey (JC). Both of us were excited and nervous before the start.

We had our clothing and equipment by the suitcase load. JC said on the morning of the prologue, "Bob, now this is the big one, the Tour de France!"

Much to my surprise the day before the start I could not believe that Arthur Metcalfe, who had ridden the Tour the year before, was trying to fit new shoe plates to his racing shoes. In those days you needed to either nail or screw the plates on yourself to the soles of the racing shoes.

Vin Denson sponsors had not provided him with new shorts, and he was looking to borrow some from the Mackenson boys who had three riders in the team.

Stage 1A was the prologue over six kilometres and was won by the French rider Charly Grosskost. Hugh Porter came in seventh at fifteen seconds behind the winner. I finished mid-field having given the six kilometres all I had.

My legs seemed to be blocked, I could not get any more out of them.

Next day, stage 1B, a one hundred- and eighty-five kilometres ride from Vittel in France to finish in Luxembourg. The stage started at an easy pace, but the last twenty kilometres was at breakneck speed in the peloton with gaps opening and closing to the finish.

Stage two. Two hundred and ten kilometres into Belgium with the Belgium team going absolutely ballistic in the last two hours of the stage resulting in Erik de Vlaeninck of Belgium taking the win.

Stage 3A was a team time trial over twenty-two kilometres.

Once again, the crowds were enormous.

The Belgium team came out top and we managed seventh place.

After a break of one and a half hours we started out on stage 3B.

One hundred and twelve kilometres in the afternoon into the famous track finish in Roubaix and over some of the famous cobbles along the way. JC and I found ourselves desperately hanging onto the peloton and at times swopping turns just to stay in contact with the rear of the race.

The stage was won by the Belgium rider Walter Godefroot.

As JC and I sat exhausted on the grass in the middle of the track, he said, "If anybody says to me you haven't got talent, I will not believe it.

Every time you did a turn it was hell, you swung over and I thought he must have blown by now, look round and you were still there."

We were then interrupted by a loud bang as my front tyre exploded, how lucky was that.

Stage four was Roubaix to Rouen in Normandy, a distance of two hundred and thirty-eight kilometres on one of the hottest days ever.

The roads were a sea of melted tar, it was like going through treacle, tar and more tar to which Jan Jansen, who was to eventually win the Tour, came alongside me and said, "Englishman, is it hot?"

To which I replied, "No, it is f---ing hot."

He did no more than ride up the edge of the peloton telling everybody how f---ing hot it was.

At the end of the stage the only way we could get the tar off our legs and arms was to get petrol and dissolve it off. It was an absolute nightmare for the mechanics as our bikes were covered in it.

Later that evening one of the teams asked, "Who told Jan Jansen it was f---ing hot?" I had to own up.

While in Rouen, I met up with some of the family who I had stayed with as an amateur there.

The following day was a split stage of one hundred and sixty-five kilometres followed, ninety minutes later, by a one hundred- and fifty-four kilometre stage. I remember vividly that trying to eat steak at five in the morning was no joke.

In the afternoon stage after some thirty kilometres, I was experiencing severe stomach cramps. I made my way back to race doctor Dumas and he gave me some ice to suck, plus a large vitamin c tablet which before consuming, I queried what was in it.

The good news was that within fifteen minutes I was almost back to normal.

My duties on the rest of the tour were to go backwards and forwards to the team car collecting bottles for our two team leaders, Barry Hoban and Michael Wright.

On stage eight I decided that I would try to lead out one of our sprinters for the finish, notably JC. The result would be a placing in the top ten for him and myself in twenty-first position.

Royan was our rest day, so we all went out and did two and a half hours at a steady pace. We had a photo shoot on the beach and the usual massage.

Mainly we spent our time laying out on our beds recovering and eating as much as possible.

Stage nine was only one hundred and thirty-seven kilometres.

Once again this was at breakneck speed due mainly to the rest day the day before. With one kilometre to go to the track finish I said to big Vin Denson, "I'll lead you out."

With that a gap appeared in front of me, and with Vin on my wheel, I gave it all I had. I entered the track in first place but as I did, a group swept past me. Unfortunately, Vin had lost my wheel just before the entrance and on my wheel had been the ultimate winner, Godefroot.

The only consolation was that JC finished in the top six of the stage.

Stage ten saw my first big crash of the tour.

After picking up bottles and progressing my way back to the bunch, on descending a hill, I had a front wheel blow out on a bend. It caused me to crash and hit the ground hard, travelling some distance and taking most of the skin of my right leg, elbow and buttocks.

After a quick front wheel change, and a chase of eighteen kilometres on my own, I regained the main peloton.

I called the race doctor for some running repairs while still on the bike but subsequently, I did not have the best night's sleep that night.

Stage eleven, Vayonne to Pau was to be a nightmare for me and ultimately, the end of my Tour de France.

Descending a hill in the middle of the main peloton and approaching a tight left-hand bend at speed, I heard a shout, and the German rider Ernest Streng came crashing into me. He took both of us over the edge of the road and down the slope beyond.

I managed to climb up to the road, but my bike was still further down the slope with the other rider. Some of the spectators managed to retrieve it for me. The ambulance stopped at the scene to assist and unfortunately the German rider had sustained a broken pelvis.

With two new wheels in my bike, I very hesitantly set off only to discover very quickly that I could not focus as I was suffering with double vision.

I was seeing two bends and two sections of road and was disorientated. Helmets were not compulsory in this era, and I had taken a decent head knock.

On top of this, I had lost the use of my hands, they were numb, with no feeling in them whatsoever. My breaking became very erratic and I was confused.

Sadly, it was time to call it a day and climb into the sag wagon after having completed fourteen stages.

After the tour, it was reported in the International Cycle Sport magazine that, "Bob Addy is another who might well have finished in Paris, but for two falls on successive days with the Pyrenees in sight. At the same time he was recovering his strength after a bout of stomach trouble. All the team worked well together and unselfishly in 'rescue operations' in time of punctures or mechanical trouble and none harder than Bob."

On returning to the UK I went to see a specialist about the last crash that had caused me to abandon my race.

The report was concussion and a badly squashed nerve in my spine, up in the neck area, which had caused numbness in both hands. The specialist told me, "You are extremely lucky that you are not in a wheelchair now."

I was very disappointed to end my Tour but thankful to be still able to race another day.

Later in the season I would finish in fifth place behind the winner Colin Lewis in the National Professional Road Race Championship. I also had a seventh place in the Tom Simpson Memorial Road race which was run for the first time following Tom's death in the Tour de France the previous year.

Bob Addy winning the Vaux Grand Prix 1969
held in the North East of England.

Riding as a Professional for Ron Kitching breaking the
London to York Solo record.

Poster of the London-York.

Photograph of Dad (George) who made me into a Champion.
John Woodburn in the background.

Scottish National Team before the Saudi Tour 1998.
The main sponsor was Giant bikes.

Team Energy before an early season Road race with Bob as the Manager.

Invitation Gentleman's two up with Dad in the
Unity Club colours in France.

Three generations of the Addy family before a Hemel Hempstead evening
16 km time trial. Jason, Dad (George), Bob and Harvey
with our red car in the background.

Personal best in Essex E72. 40km time trial 52 minutes 14 seconds riding in Hemel Hempstead colours and wet weather again.

Crystal Palace finish beating from left to right Roger Claridge, Arthur Metcalfe, Derek Green, Colin Lewis and the winner Bob Addy about to celebrate.

Tour de France 1968. A welcome spray from someone's
hose pipe on a Very hot day into Rouen France.

London-Battle and back. First year riding for Holdsworth, putting out some pain in echelon in the crosswind.

Finish at Herne Hill, West Coast Masters club. Bob,(third from the left in Black) and the winner by half a wheel in Western Australia.

Road race on the attack and going solo onto win the
Club Championship. Australia 2015.

My last time trial aged 75 years in Western Australia
riding a bike generously loaned from Glen Parker Cycles in Perth.

Leading into the final corner giving it a lot of effort in a criterium,
Kewdale, Western Australia.
Alison Dyson trying to hold onto my back wheel for the finish.

Team Energy with Simon Bray holding his National Championship jersey
with the rest of the team and staff.
Bob on the extreme left in Yellow, the team manager.

Bob and Roger Hammond, after Bob had helped Roger to win the
Great Britain National Professional Road Title in Wales 2004.

Wendy handing up a sponge to Bob on Brill Hill in the U.K.
Having punctured, changed his tyre and chasing to get back to the leaders.
Next lap round, Bob won at top of Brill Hill.

Bobs celebration of his 80th birthday with family taken at his home.
Courtesy of Keef Hickey.

Bob at the front of his home in Western Australia.
Still fitting into his 1964 Olympic uniform at the age of 81.

CHAPTER 21

1969 - THE VAUX GRAND PRIX

The Vaux Grand Prix was, in its time, the UK's top one-day event and was run on ten consecutive occasions from 1961 to 1970. The winners of the last five races were as follows:

1966: Les West amateur, second in the World Amateur Road Championship, fourth in the World Professional Road Race Championship and Tour of Britain Winner.

1967: Michael Wright, professional. Stage wins in Tour de France and Tour of Spain.

1968: Vin Denson, professional. Stage winner in the Tour of Italy. Winner of the Tour of Luxembourg.

1969: Bob Addy, professional. Former Amateur British Champion and Tour de France rider.

1970: Barry Hoban, professional. Stage wins in the Tour de France.

The 1969 Vaux Grand Prix was the richest single day race held in the British Isles and had built up a reputation as the hardest on the British calendar.

It attracted tens of thousands of spectators from the Northeast of Britain to watch the race over the bleak moors with total climbing of 3,500 meters.

This was a truly British classic and was run over a distance of one hundred and eighty-five kilometres. It was an event I had wanted to win for a long time.

I'd finished ninth in the first edition of the event held in 1961 when I was 20-years old. My next appearance would be some seven years later in 1968, when I finished seventh, having missed the early break when feeling in exceptional form.

I determined that the 1969 Vaux was going to be mine. I trained hard, had good form and was focused on the race. I was confident that I could perform at a top level having in recent times competed well in the company of the likes of Felice Gimondi, Lucien Aimar, winners of the Tour de France and many other top professionals.

Come the evening before the event, Wendy and I were looking for somewhere to eat. We went into a hotel where all the officials from the race were staying and asked the restaurant if we could have a steak dinner.

"Sorry, all the steak dinners had been taken by the Vaux officials and organizers of the race." Was the reply! Typical!

On the day of the race the weather was overcast.

Barry Hoban was over from the continent to ride with Graham Gilmore and Ward Janssens as his helpers in the race.

After only twenty-four kilometres a break of seven of us got clear. Working well together, by the second lap we were down to four, having dropped Vin Denson, Pete Chisman and Bill Painter.

I then had my first puncture but, with a swift change I got back to the lead group very quickly. At this stage the gap back to the main peloton was four minutes.

Halfway through the race saw the first of several thunderstorms with torrential rain of biblical proportions. We were unable to see more than a few metres in front of us. And I punctured again!

I was on a super day and again regained the leaders after a short chase. I felt wonderful, as though I had no chain and no pain in the legs. I was floating on air.

At Hill End on the third lap, Goz Goodman cracked.

At the start of our final lap, Ward Janssens was dropped.

The thunderstorm continued, we could see the lightning all around us, the smell of burnt gorse on the moors and the heavy rain continued.

The last time up the long climb of Bollihope Common, West Mason, who was the only other rider left with me said, "Bob, you have dropped Janssens, and I can't keep up with the pace you are setting."

I thought to myself, "Bugger, I've still got some forty-four kilometres to go."

I accelerated away from Wes and would be forty-five seconds clear of him as I went over the top of Bollihope.

I saw Wendy at the side of the road as I went over the top of the climb, standing with the rest of the wives of the Holdsworth team and the Team manager Roy Thame. Roy turned to Wendy and asked, "How's Bob going?"

"Very well." Was her reply.

Surely, he should have known being the team manager!

With the rain still hammering down, I pressed on.

This was going to be my Vaux race win at last.

A car of officials sped by with Len Unwin, one of the British Cycling Federation officials shouting encouragement and giving me the thumbs up. No sooner had they passed when, bang, another puncture, my third of the race.

This time it was a rear wheel.

I must have hit one of the many stones and rocks that were being washed across the roads, which were now like rivers. It seemed the rain was horizontal, stinging my arms and legs as I pulled to a stop.

Immediately behind was the service car for the race with Harry Hall, one of the best mechanics you could wish for on board. A new bike swap and off I went.

With some eight kilometres to go to the finish, Harry drove alongside me and said, "Bob, your bike is ready. It would look better for you to finish on your Holdsworth."

"How much time have I got to the next rider?" I asked.

"At least three minutes."

"Let's do it."

On the last climb the road was still extremely wet but thankfully it had stopped raining. My dream from 1961 was about to come true, despite three punctures and two bike changes.

I swept over the line with both arms aloft, Winner of the 1969 Vaux Grand Prix.

In second place was Wes Mason at three minutes, twenty-five seconds. Third place went to Ward Janssens at four minutes, fifteen seconds and Barry Hoban, forth at five minutes, thirty-five seconds.

This would be the biggest winning margin in the history of the race.

Holding my race number of thirteen aloft, I climbed onto the top of the podium. Barry Hoban was not a happy rider despite getting start money to come over for the race. He commented to the press that the English based riders refused to chase down the break and they were nothing but a load of cowboys.

Well, this one rode away, not quite into the sunset but I was the top gun on the day. Oh, what a feeling.

The main headline in Cycling Weekly was, "Addy obeys the Roadman's commandment: Never ignore an early break."

"When the Holdsworth/Campagnolo man crossed the line alone after one of the greatest rides the race had seen, he must surely have carried some justifiable glee of memories of the days when he seemed unwanted and considered to have had his day."

In 1970, I had numerous high placings, especially in stage races. However, I was still very much a domestic in the team and only managed to finish sixteenth in the National Professional Road Championship. I competed in many criteriums that year, which wasn't my forte. While I had a substantial amount of top ten finishes, I only managed to stand on the podium on a handful of occasions.

1971 was a year of nothing but criteriums again.

When we had road races and especially stage races, I would be in my element in those events. I had continued to prepare carefully, spending time and effort in the correct use of carb-loading and protein use, a valuable tool for any athlete.

I finished fifth in the National Professional Road Race Title despite feeling some cramp towards the end. The riders who finished in front of me had good preparation in their legs due to having just returned from the Tour of Switzerland. I had been in a group of twelve riders with the winner being Danny Horton, winning on his own by one minute.

I would be the top Holdsworth rider, with Colin and Les also in the same twelve rider group.

At the end of the season, I would leave the team that I had helped create with Roy Thame. It was time for new adventures.

CHAPTER 22

THE RON KITCHING PROFESSIONAL ROAD TEAM

The newly formed Ron Kitching team saw me appointed as the captain, having also been in that position with the Holdsworth.

The colours of the team were a very distinctive green and black.

Once again, my forte was to be in road races and in particular the Tour of the North seven-day stage race which was part sponsored by Ron Kitching.

In one of the stages of that tour, Graham Moore also in our team, won it and I took out the bunch sprint for second, much to the delight of Ron. I was to finish the race in eighth place overall.

A week after the end of the Tour of the North, I was going to attempt the Road Record Association Record from London to York which had been set by Shake Ernshaw and despite many attempts over the years by some of the top time trialists of the day, it had stood for nearly forty years.

When I asked Ron about having a team car to follow me for the event he said, "Aye lad, I'll meet you halfway down the track and follow you from there."

"You have got to be joking mate, what happens if I have mechanical problems before halfway?"

Instead, I had my brother-in-law Mick Shea follow with Den Mills who helped with the schedule.

On all record attempts you had to have a regulation timekeeper or observer in the car as well. It was also a requirement to notify the Road Records Association seven days before you were going to attempt a record. This allowed observers to get out along the route to ensure there was no drafting or pacing being done or riding in a vehicle.

On the day I arrived at the main London Post Office at 6:00 in the morning for the start. There was a slight breeze early on, which later became a very strong cross / tail wind. The schedule was to beat the record by around twelve minutes, and I felt very confident I could achieve this due to the super form I had from the Tour of the North stage race.

I scorched through the one-hundred-and-sixty kilometre mark in under four hours.

I was going so well that the helpers in the following car became concerned that I was already well up on schedule. At this point of the ride down came the heavy showers, my type of weather.

I always did a lot of my rides when the weather was inclement, so I could handle this without a problem.

Part way along the A1 (the major highway from London to York) there was a time trial in progress and at one of the turn offs from the A1, the Marshall came into the middle of the road and tried to drag me off the bike and put me down the slip road. Luckily, I managed to avoid him and carry on.

Forty kilometres from York, Ron Kitching was standing on the side of the road. As I approached him, he shouted, "Bloody hell lad, you're going to absolutely smash the record."

The finish was outside the York Main Post Office. All record attempts started and finished at the Post Office on a one-way attempt.

The record was mine, breaking the previous record by forty-one minutes and forty-one seconds at an average speed of nearly forty-one kilometres an hour. Total distance, three hundred and eighteen kilometres.

On the same day, there was the annual York Cycle rally with trade stands and grass track racing events being held. With a quick change of clothes into fresh racing kit, I had put in my bag in anticipation of smashing the record, Ron Kitching had a big trade stand and an announcement was made to the crowds that I was signing autographs as the new Record Holder of the London to York.

Years later Paul Donohue, who became one of the top frame builders in the UK and built frames for many famous cyclists who achieved great things, contacted me to say that he was just a kid starting out in cycling when he saw me at the Ron Kitching stand. He still had a signed autograph from that day. He told me that through the generosity of my autograph that day and the further inspiration I had provided, I had contributed to the parts of the jigsaw that shaped British cycling into what it is today.

Twenty-two years later, in 1994, Glen Longland would break my London to York record.

Later in the 1972 season, I had a third placing in the Tom Simpson Memorial race which was now becoming a Classic around his village of Harworth in Nottinghamshire.

This was followed by another record attempt, the London to Bath and back. Despite the adverse weather, I would add this attempt to my successes.

The day coincided with the London six-day Cycle race that was being held at Wembley Arena and Ron Kitching had a table in the centre of the track.

When I sent word into him that I had broken the record he invited me in and informed me that the organizer, Ron Webb wanted him to pay for me to ride round the track announcing I had just broken the record, to which Ron retorted, "No way mate." Hence it didn't happen. Bearing in mind that Ron was an extremely successful businessman, a Yorkshire man and a bit tight on the purse strings!

In the following year, my last year as a professional, I successfully lowered the Bath to London and back record, taking ten minutes off my previous ride in better weather conditions. Ron said that as I had broken my own record, he would only pay me half the bonus money.

CHAPTER 23

RETIREMENT FROM CYCLE RACING

In 1973, I took over my first bike shop in Ickenham, Middlesex.

It followed a casual conversation with Bert Rayner when I had asked if he had ever thought of selling his business.

"I've been trying to sell it for a while," he replied.

He put some figures together and we bought the shop and the stock.

***

Wendy started working in the shop whilst looking after our two small boys. Jason was about two-and-a-half- and Harvey only four months old at the time.

My days would start with a twenty-two kilometre ride to the track teaching alongside John Austin at Paddington, and a similar format at Herne Hill. I would leave the track to ride back to the shop arriving around three thirty in the afternoon.

On Tuesday and Thursday evenings I would ride an extra fifteen kilometres home, take our car back to Kilburn, take a keep fit class for cyclists and a football team, before eventually arriving home at 10:00 in the evening.

On the other days I would work at the shop until nine in the evening doing bike repairs.

Friday was my day off from the track, spent solely in the shop as was Saturday, leaving Sunday free with Wendy and our sons.

CHAPTER 24

RETURNED BACK TO AMATEUR RACING

In the event of retiring from the professional ranks, there was a mandatory requirement that a rider not compete for two years before he could apply for an amateur license.

I returned to competition with a mixture of road races, time trials and evening track racing at Paddington. My best results came with two stages and a second placing in the Luton Wheelers two-day round Dunstable, which I won overall.

I had another first in the Wild Hill Road race in Hertfordshire, a win in the Hertfordshire Time trial of forty-eight kilometres and returning to the Bath Road Hilly eighty kilometres event, finishing fourth.

I also picked up numerous evening time trials and track wins.

**

In 1977 it was much of the same; wins in time trials, road racing and excelling on a number of occasions on the track at Paddington.

In 1978, I changed clubs and rode for the Hillingdon Cycling Club. The main reason for this was that the clubroom was in the basement of my shop where I stored my excess new bikes.

Friday evenings would mean the room had to be cleared for the club meeting and from a business point of view, it proved to be a good move.

That year I decided to concentrate on the British Best All-rounder Time Trial Championship.

The Championship was made up of three time trials over eighty kilometres, one hundred and sixty kilometres and a twelve-hour event where the rider covers as many kilometres as possible in the time.

I ended up with one 1:47:30 for the eighty kilometres, 3:52:18 for the one hundred and sixty kilometres and a total distance of three hundred and fifty-six kilometres in twelve hours, which placed me third overall in the championship.

The winner was John Woodburn. Pete Wells was second and my mate, Clive Pugh came fifth. All of us were from the West London area and had been out on my training runs.

In 1984, riding in the one hundred and sixty kilometres Time Trial National Championship, I would finish in sixth place from a field of one hundred and twenty riders with a time of 3:57:57.

The following year, I improved one place to finish in fifth place with a time of three hours, fifty-five minutes, fifty-three seconds.

At the age of forty-four I attempted to do the British, "Best All-rounder" with the Hemel Club which I had rejoined.

Recording 1:48:56 over eighty kilometres, 3:51:40 over one hundred and sixty kilometres and three hundred and sixty kilometres in twelve hours, I finished seventh overall.

All these events were ridden using standard configuration road bikes and no aero equipment.

CHAPTER 25

TEAM ENERGY (DURACELL/LUCOZADE) 1995/1996

In 1995, I was approached by Ian Goodhew to join Team Energy as a manager. Ian was extremely good on the organization of the team, second to none, but after a few races, the riders requested that they wanted me as their sole manager at races.

Wendy joined the team and became the social secretary. In that capacity she got onto Duracell and asked if they had any merchandise to hand out at races and to give to members of the social club. She also did a monthly newsletter on the team, detailing where they would be racing next.

We were most surprised when Duracell sent boxes and boxes of pink bunnies with white shirts and green shorts on. There must have been over a thousand of them, plus a small number of battery-operated ones complete with a drum. These were handed to our team member when on the podiums.

All of this worked well, the success of the team continued in the run-up to the National Road Race Championship and we were one of the first teams to make a clean sweep of 1st, 2nd and 3rd in the Welsh Open Premier Road Race.

Being that most of the races beforehand were shorter distances than the National, I instructed them to race extremely aggressive and not to worry about where they would finish. Then, immediately after the finish, the riders would do an extra eighty kilometres with the team car following, ending up at a pub where they could get changed and have refreshments before continuing their journey home.

At the time I was phoning one of the riders, Simon Bray, a couple of times a week to see how his training was going and to give him a motivation talk.

The National Championship was run over a flat course. Towards the end, Simon, who had won the National before on a very hilly course round Buxton, (the same course where I had won my national title), took off with a few kilometres to go and won in style. This showed his undoubted talent to win on all types of courses and subsequently gave me some bargaining power to get in touch with the organizer of the Herald Sun Tour in Australia, John Craven. He was very generous and arranged to part sponsor our air travel, due in part to us having the current British Champion on our team.

The following year, the team was even stronger. We managed many wins throughout the British and Irish races. Again, the team followed the same winning formula in the build up to the National Road Race title which had now become an open title, professional/amateur. The likes of Chris Boardman and the continental professionals came over for the event.

I had kept Simon and David Rand on their toes with regular phone calls and pep talks prior to the race.

"We must have numbers in that early break," I would tell them.

This happened when a fifteen-rider break escaped with four being from our team. The instructions were that they must have a five-minute lead by the time they hit the final finishing circuit.

Three riders sacrificed themselves with David as the protected rider. Simon, the defending Champion, was still back in the main peloton.

On the start of the finishing circuit, the lead was four and a half minutes. The break progressively fell apart until only three riders were left out in front. The time gap had continually come down, but we also now had Simon on his own, having taken off from the peloton. He managed to close the gap to within touching distance as the three riders started sprinting for the line.

Dave took the Victory from Andy Naylor and David Cook in third place.

Team Energy had finished first and fourth and yet again the British Road Race Champion was in the team.

One blight on all of this was that before the race, the then England team manager stated that, "Whoever won the title would go to the Olympics." Despite the statement and many phone calls and letters that followed, David was left out of the team. A huge injustice.

John Herety, who at the time was looking after the Professional Kodak

Team, had commented on a number of occasions that the method I had employed of making the riders doing extra kilometres, "Will kill off some of your riders by doing that." At the finish he came up and shook my hand and said, "You've done it again, National Champion in the team, well done." A short while after he was to become the British National Road Coach.

Having the National Champion again enabled me to take the team to the Herald Sun Tour in Australia for a second time, along with guest riders Andy Naylor and Roger Hammond. We enjoyed some good results during the race, the best being Roger finishing second to Robbie McEwen on the last day.

Sadly, the following year, the team folded due to the main sponsors, Duracell and Lucozade, pulling out. This was disappointing due to the enormous amount of publicity we had received and on being the most successful team in the United Kingdom at the time.

For myself it had been a great experience with a group of very talented riders who gave their all for me as their team manager.

CHAPTER 26

THE MARLBORO TOUR OF THE PHILLIPINES - 1997

At the beginning of April, 1997, I had a meeting with Alan Rushton and Mick Bennett to discuss going to the Philippines for the sixteen-day Marlboro Stage race.

The idea was for it to become a U.C.I. (Union Cycliste Internationale) rated event. However, to achieve this it had to be up to a certain standard. It was believed that by taking several ex-professional riders with experience, both as riders and managers, to look after some of the teams during the tour it would assist with the protocols required.

The riders to be involved were myself, having just finished looking after Team Energy, Colin Lewis, Phil Corley, Dave Mitchell and Mick Ives. For our expertise we would have all our flights, accommodation and generous expenses covered for the twenty-one days we were to be there.

We arrived three days before the start, the first stages were to be held on the island of Mindanao, where we were introduced to our teams. I was to manage the regional team from Mindanao and, as Alan said at the time, "It's record on the Tour had previously been one of the worst, and as you are the most experienced manager, I am designating you to them."

In total I had the seven riders in the team, another Philippine manager, a driver and two mechanics, one of which I nicknamed 'The Bandit' because he came from northern Mindanao where most of the rebel factions lived.

One of the biggest shocks on meeting the riders from my team was their equipment, bikes and clothing. I asked them why they had different coloured socks, and why their handlebar tape did not match from one side to another. In answer I was told, "It's cheaper just to get one sock or piece of tape if you come off. It doesn't matter about the colour."

On the first day I followed the riders in the car for about ninety kilometres. I had to stop them on a few occasions to try and get them to roll through instead of sprinting against each other up the road.

I soon became referred to as, "Mr Bob."

During that first ride we came across some young lads, about eight to ten years old, with carts made up of a platform of wood, four pram wheels held together with rope and a piece of wood attached to the front wheels to enable them to steer. On the cart, a big container of water which was to be filled up at the bottom of an eight kilometre long hill. Their method of getting to the top was to wait for a passing truck, quickly hook the rope around the rear bumper, while it was still moving, and then get dragged to the top of the climb where they would unhook the rope and empty the water into a huge container. For each successful trip they got paid.

However, the risk of hooking onto a moving truck on the ride up was nothing compared to coming down such a hill with only a piece of wood applied to the back tyre for breaking while also steering with the other hand.

My riders told me that there had been many accidents with these boys hitting trucks coming up the opposite way.

***

Back at the hotel after our first training day, I asked what the riders usually took to eat and drink during a race. They answered that they would go to the local store and buy a sandwich and they just had water in their drinking bottles. In preparation for the tour, I had brought some energy bars and energy powder for the bottles. They could not believe the affect it had on them and the amount of energy it produced.

One of the biggest hurdles to overcome was that in the past they would always line up for the start of the race in very hot and humid conditions at least ninety minutes beforehand. It was so bad that one day the managers went down into the reception area of the hotel we were staying in and formed a human chain to stop the riders from going out so early.

The race itself was extremely fast. The only way that they knew how to race was to attack from the start, all the way to the finish, nothing but attack, attack, attack, until they blew up, day after day. We made the effort to educate them on alternative tactics, which assisted with better results.

On one day in particular, a rider from our team was in a breakaway of eight riders. All of them were in the top fifteen overall of the race. My rider at the time was lying in thirtieth place. With fifty kilometres to go they had a four-minute advantage, so I had our driver pull up alongside him and told the rider to sit on. "Don't do any work until eight to ten kilometres to go. When you do go through, very easy."

At the finish he managed to come in a very close second.

"Mr Bob," he said as he hugged me, tears running down his face, "You have won me a lot of money for my family."

It turned out to be equivalent of nearly three and a half months' wages. I felt so good, it was if I had won it myself.

Every day in the tour, the last hour of every stage was broadcast on the television while the whole of the stage was being reported on the radio. I asked my rider, "Will your wife have seen you on your television?"

"I don't have one, but my uncle's friend in the place I live has a television, so she'll be round there with the two children."

The team also managed a third place on a stage, much to everyone's delight as this was better than they had ever done in previous tours.

On one evening the mechanic said to me, "It is urgent, you must have a look at one of the rider's bikes. We have a very big problem. The front forks have a crack in them."

When we told the rider of this his reply was, "Oh, I know about it and have painted over it two weeks ago, it will be okay."

That evening I managed to get a new pair of forks from the Hong Kong team at no cost despite our rider saying he couldn't afford it.

It concerned me to think that the riders in the race were descending down the mountains at over eighty kilometres per hour with a pair of front forks held together with paint.

Most of the accommodation was very good but on a couple of days I had to make sure I had my shoes on because the floor was covered in cockroaches, especially at night, much to the amusement of the rest of our team.

Our riders could not believe the luxury of some of the hotels we stayed in, having never stayed in anything like that before.

On one stage, I'd been pre-warned that after forty kilometres the roads had been dug up and left with massive holes and rocks for about six kilometres further on. That evening I went out to have a look with one of the mechanics from our team.

On getting to the site, it was like a bomb had gone off. We managed to get through and plotted a route. For the first two kilometres, move to the right-hand side of the track, for the next one kilometre move to the left-hand side and for the final three kilometres stay in the middle and slightly to the right.

On getting back I told the riders at the hotel that at the far end of this section of road our luggage minibus would be parked with spares in case of punctures. Also, two kilometres before the bad road there was a very big bridge on their left-hand side. One of the riders had to put his hand up to indicate he had mechanical trouble, that way I would be called up on the radio to move up to the first car behind the commissaire instead of being fifteenth in the convoy. The other instructions to the team were that when they saw the bridge they had to get to the front of the group.

This all worked like a dream.

At the end of the six kilometres, we had five riders in a break of thirteen. Unfortunately, there was still over ninety kilometres to go and they were caught twenty kilometres from the finish.

This was something I passed onto Roger Hammond when he rode the Paris Roubaix, as his team at the time was in a similar situation, just before the notorious stretch through the forest. It meant his team car went through as the third car and overall the tactic worked brilliantly. His manager asked, "Whose idea was that?" To which Roger said, "Bob Addy's." Subsequently in the years after they didn't let the cars through that section.

One of the things I also introduced to my Philippine team was that after every stage I got the riders to immerse their bodies, from waist down, in dustbins filled with iced water for ten minutes. Some of the other managers said, "Bob, you will kill them." But apart from a few yells, all agreed they felt good afterwards.

A few years later most of the Tour de France team buses had caught on to my idea and had iced baths in the back.

The other thing I got them to do was to warm down after having had their recovery drink.

Another big shock was that after the race when I had our final meeting, the boys said, "Mr. Bob we have something to give you for all the help and advice you have given us."

They handed me over £50 which to them was the equivalent of six or seven weeks' wages. I flatly refused the extremely kind gift, despite their protests.

I would hear later that one of the other managers had been offered even more than I had by his team. He took it.

What a scumbag.

The other thing that sticks in my mind was that on the last day of the race, on the way down to the reception area, it was absolutely heaving with a lot of men in suits milling around. I asked our manager what was happening. He said that's the money lenders. The majority of the riders had to borrow from them to get their bikes ready for the tour, now they wanted their money back or to work out a payment plan.

This made me understand why they raced so hard and yet despite their hardships, as I saw them, they were the happiest people I have ever met in the cycling world.

It turned out to be a very humbling experience for me, combined also with the grief I was still dealing with after my dad had passed away just before I had left for the Philippines.

CHAPTER 27

RETIREMENT TO SCOTLAND AND THE
SCOTTISH NATIONAL CYCLE TEAM

In 1998 at the age of fifty-seven, Wendy and I retired from the cycling business to a little village called Glencaple near Dumfries, Scotland. It was the birthplace of Wendy's mother and she still had relatives living there.

Wendy's late grandfather, James Wilson was the Head Gamekeeper to the late Duke of Norfolk, so Wendy's family were well known in the small village.

We were permitted to purchase a block of land from the Duke's daughter, Lady Mary Mumford and build a house on the banks of the River Nith.

We grew to know Lady Mary very well through our family connection and she knew that we had owned two bike shops in England previously.

She asked Wendy if she would run the village shop for her as the current tenant had done a runner owing an enormous amount of money.

At first Wendy turned her down but then Lady Mary tugged at her heart strings saying the only shop in the village would close if she could not find suitable help. After talking it over with me we decided to take on the challenge and so another chapter began.

Within a year of taking the shop on, business was booming so much so that Lady Mary extended the shop which doubled it in size.

That same year the small village shop with post office attached took second prize in the best run village shop in Scotland.

Shortly after I arrived in Scotland, the Scottish Cycle Union asked me if I would be interested in being the Manager of the Scottish National Cycle Team. The other person to be interviewed for the job was Brian Smith, a double National Road Champion, also an ex-professional rider.

During the interview I was informed that it was a non-salary position and that the team only had a total of £5,000. This amount was granted from the lottery and based on the performance of the Scottish Team, which at the time had appalling results, hence the low amount of funding.

I had to hire a car most weekends, pay for accommodation, travel and jerseys. We had a squad of twelve riders of which six would be riding in events plus, on some of the races, there would be myself as manager, a masseur and a mechanic, a total of nine people.

I suggested to the riders that if they paid for their own Scottish jerseys that we would be able to go to two more events down in England where the majority of the big races were held, to which they all agreed.

As a result of getting the appointment I started reaching out to my many contacts in the sport to get sponsorship for the team. We raised close to £125,000 in the way of ten Giant bikes, clothing, tyres, sports drinks, sunglasses and other consumables.

I also managed to do a deal with a local hire car company so that we had very reasonable rates. This was beneficial as on most weekends when travelling down south to England we were doing between six to nine hundred kilometres of travel.

I also arranged, through British Aerospace and the Saudi Government, an all-expenses paid (for six riders and three officials) a training camp at Abhar.

The accommodation was at a brand-new sports centre with a great range of facilities including a swimming pool, and football pitch. Situated at nearly 3,000 metres high, this was ideal for three weeks of altitude training. On most days the riders would descend to sea level to do their training and return back up to sleep at altitude. We also went to several functions with British Aerospace and the Saudi Arabian Government. The following year we returned to Saudi for a seven-day stage race.

On returning to Scotland, we found that most of the riders had benefited from the altitude training, and this was seen in some very good results in the Premier series of races, mostly held in England.

One of our riders was serving in the British Army and I wrote a letter to his Commanding Officer, stating that the soldier had an extremely good chance of representing Scotland in the Commonwealth Games. I requested if it would be possible for him to have some time off for training. Within a week a reply came back. The Army were willing to grant him the time off and only required him to do one afternoon a week (four hours work). The rest of the time was for training.

Despite me arranging all this for him and supplying a brand-new bike and clothing, he complained that the bike he received was the wrong size.

I exchanged the bike, but he was still not happy. He complained that the chain was slightly rusty, and the bike had been used, which, being the spare bike that had been on the of top of the service vehicle, was correct.

He reported back to the President of the Scottish Cycle Union who duly phoned me to say that some of the riders had reported that they were not happy with the Michelin tyres (which were being supplied free of charge).

I replied, "Well that's what's on the spare wheels we keep in the car, so if they puncture, I'll drive straight past them then!"

The other thing he brought up in the conversation was that the sports and recovery drinks were not to the riders' liking.

This time I said, "It doesn't matter as long as they have the sponsors bottle on the bike. They could have whatever they liked in it."

"Well that would be deceiving the sponsor," said the President.

I thought, but didn't say, how on earth can you win!

Another subject that arose was that some of the riders did not like travelling back with me in the car, especially when I turned a tape recorder on of what had happened during the race as I was following in the team car. In some cases, either praising or suggesting they could have done things a dam sight better, during the race.

I defended my position by outlining how I only saw them once every two weeks or so and it was best that after the event they learn immediately from some of their mistakes.

The second year we had the same amount of sponsorship but still limited to £5,000 from the Scottish Cycle Union. This time I managed, through my contacts, to get us an all-expenses paid trip to South Africa, where we rode several events including a stage race of seven days.

Following our racing commitments, Alistair Kay, nicknamed the jockey because of his small size, was offered the opportunity to ride for Barlo World, the same team that Chris Froome and Gareth Thomas would later ride for. To my amazement Alistair, turned them down.

Immediately after South Africa we went back to Saudi with five Scottish riders plus an Irish rider, Paul Griffin, who turned out to be one of the most professional and dedicated riders I had come across.

We took three officials down there, one of whom was my son Harvey, as the mechanic. The trip was three weeks in Saudi at altitude and included a seven-day stage race. One of the stages was won by Alistair Kay, being a solo winner on a very long climb of twenty-four kilometres.

It was Easter by the time we returned, and the team competed in a big four-day Premier stage race in Scotland. My role was again that of manager, looking after the under-23 team and a six-man senior team.

The under-23s having returned from South Africa and Saudi dominated the event much to the surprise of the semi-professional English teams and all the Scottish riders. They went from strength to strength during the year and were producing the best results for over 15 years in events both in Scotland and more importantly in the Premier events in England. I was also the first manager to introduce radios for the riders.

With so much success the National Lottery fund managers decided that the Scottish Cycle Team needed better funding to enable them to ride in more events and to assist in the build-up to the forthcoming Commonwealth Games, due to be held in Manchester the following year.

The budget was increased to from £5,000 to £80,000, also a car and a salary of £40,000 for the manager. I applied for the position.

The Scottish Cycle Union gave the job to the person who had previously looked after the team at the 1998 Commonwealth Games in Kuala Lumpur, Malaysia. I was surprised, as during those games, the road riders had booked to go on a Safari on the same day as the road race and told the manager that they were going to abandon the race to do so, which they did. In my opinion they'd been completely out of control. But perhaps memories were short. Whatever the thinking, the Scottish Cycle Union appointed him back to lead the team in Manchester 2002.

He had the audacity to ask me for all the sponsorship contacts and if I would accompany him in the team car to advise him on how I directed the riders. I told him to get stuffed.

Likewise, I declined when he asked me to carry on with a training camp that had been arranged in Scotland, but that was due to be held two weeks after he took over.

I had also arranged for riders to travel to the Isle of Man for a big international event followed by the international road race in the Cotswold. The accommodation, meals and travel expenses had been negotiated previously by me. All of which was messed up by the new manager in arriving at the accommodation at 1:30 in the morning before the race scheduled for the same day. Subsequently the Scottish Team lost a lot of sponsorship plus depletion of lottery funding.

A few years later, in 2005, at the age of 64, I left the UK with Wendy and we emigrated to Western Australia. I thought I was done with cycling. Happily, I was wrong.

CHAPTER 28

RACING IN AUSTRALIA

I started to race with the Peel Club as well as the West Coast Masters on most weekends starting in 2006, a year after settling in Australia. Some of my notable results were in the 2009 Tour Down Under Veterans series. I finished second in the National Time Trial and Criterium Championships and won the Road Race.

In the National Veteran series (for age group 65-69) I became the Time Trial, Criterium and Road Race Champion, to become the only rider to have won both British and Australian Road National titles.

In my local West Australian State Titles, I was first in the road race, second in the time trial and third in the over-55 State road race at the age of sixty-eight. I'm fortunate that in every year I have contested the Veterans National titles, I've always ended on the podium.

At the age of 72, I was still racing in A-grade races with the West Coast Masters and in B-grade open events. I stopped racing in 2017, at the age of 76, but continued to ride mainly with my mate, Brian Buck, doing between three hundred to three hundred and fifty kilometres per week.

During my time in Australia, I've had several requests from riders to coach them which I have done and with as much success as I had in Britain and Europe.

My main method of coaching has always been on a one-on-one basis.

The efforts have resulted in a World Championship for Richard Barville and in the ladies, a World Championship and a 2nd place for Cass Higgs.

CHAPTER 29

TYLER HAMILTON
TOUR DE TRUTH

In August 2013, it came to my notice that the ex-professional rider, Tyler Hamilton was on a World Tour and coming to Perth to explain how he became involved with, and the methods he used in, cheating the drug control protocols along with his team mates, most notably, Lance Armstrong.

The breakfast talk was held at the Perth Convention and Exhibition Centre which had an audience of over 500 people. I went along with my two sons, Jason and Harvey. We arrived at the venue to be seated at a round table of 15 people. The tables nearest the stage where Hamilton was speaking from were taken up by corporate bosses.

At the end of his talk, outlining how and when he indulged in his quest to be one of the best riders at the time along with his teammates, the compere said to the audience that a mobile microphone would come around so that we could put questions to Hamilton. I had previously told the people on my table that when this happened, I was desperate to get hold of that mic.

As the roaming mic came close to our table, one of the men seated next to me managed to get hold of it and quickly passed it over. I stood up, introduced myself and quickly outlined some of the races I had competed in which were similar in stature to Hamilton's.

Then I said, "You have to ask, who is the winner? You're getting paid to be a liar and a cheater here today."

I said that I had been forced out of the sport because I refused to dope and I questioned the ethics of Hamilton profiting from more than a decade of cheating to win. It was a point which wasn't well received by the audience but one which Hamilton said he could not completely disagree with.

He was one of the guys who got burned, and it was he who should have been angry, and he had every reason to be.

On leaving the venue and walking onto the escalator, a group of people had gathered at the bottom looking up at my sons and I.

"Don't worry Dad, we are right here with you," they said.

When we reached the bottom of the escalator the group moved forward and started congratulating me for my remarks and stated that this was exactly what they were thinking at the time but didn't have the bottle to stand up and confront him, adding that I had the credentials to do it.

After much hand shaking, and as we moved away, my boys said that it was good to hear and well worth getting it off my chest.

CHAPTER 30

SOME OF THE WELL-KNOWN RIDERS THAT I HAVE HELPED IN THEIR RACING CAREERS

Roger Hammond

I got to know Roger Hammond and his parents Beryl and Stu, through my shop in Ickenham, but also at the time racing with and against Stu.

I went out on a number of training rides with Roger and looked after him in the Junior Tour of Wales where I was the manager of the West London Juniors which was made up from many riders from the Hemel.

One good bit of advice I gave to Roger on that race was on the last big climb, on the last day, he had to make that his finishing effort which he duly did, taking advantage of being an extremely good descender down to the finish.

He won the stage and the overall event. Something I am sure he has passed onto the riders he now looks after in his role as manager.

My son Harvey, who was in that Junior team, also did the same tactic coming over the top of the hill in fifth place which placed him in sixth overall.

Roger was one of the guest riders in the team that I took out to the Herald Sun Tour. After the last stage where he finished second to Robbie McEwen, we had a very long chat about him becoming a professional as he'd had a number of offers.

One of the things I said to him was you must try and lose a few kilos through the winter and maybe don't do too many cycle cross events in Europe, which for Roger meant him cutting back on his start money being the then British National Cyclocross champion and ex-World Junior Champion.

This led me to helping Roger on a number of occasions by phoning him at his home in Belgium.

He became the first British professional at the time to use an altitude tent, icing on stage races, pre-race food, cutting out caffeine before races and using it in races. After race recovery drink, elevated bed and many more tips that I offered to him. We were constantly in touch before the big races such as Roubaix and Flanders.

It was a wonderful journey with the two time British Professional Road Champion who was later to become a top professional road manager, using some of the many things we had learnt and shared together.

David Miller.

David Miller would ride as a junior in Team Energy. I had met him before at an evening sixteen kilometre time trial run by the High Wycombe club where I managed to beat him by a few seconds. Later, as a member of the team, he came to me and asked my advice on how he should race the National Junior forty kilometre time trial, a distance which he had never done before.

The advice was that there is only one way, flat out, as hard as you can all the way. The result was he won it easily.

At the end of the season he left Team Energy and went to Europe as a first year senior, eventually becoming one of the top professionals.

Graham Obree.

I met Graham Obree when he was a young junior in a time trial in Scotland when Wendy and I were on holiday. Upon finishing the race, I was informed that I had done a great ride and had finished second to the junior, Graham Obree, who had beaten me by a few seconds.

A few years later when he became the World Hour Record holder, he got in touch with me and recalled what I had said to him in Scotland, "If you keep at it you could become one of the best riders around."

This he did many times over at world level.

Matt Stephens.

On one of our club evening sixteen kilometre time trials, Matt Stephens's mum came up to me and asked, "Can't you let Matt win one of these?"

To which I answered, "No way, he's got to earn it."

Matt was an up and coming junior at the time and sure enough, he went on to earn many a victory.

A couple of years later he was to start one minute behind me in the evening time trial and caught me after just eight kilometres. Not to be outdone I stayed with him until the last rise before the finish and jumped him to finish some three seconds in front making it look as though he had failed to catch me, much to his disgust.

One of my famous training runs was from the train station at Bovingdon. Matt decided to come out on his mountain bike. The ride took us out towards Bicester and returned on the Bunbury Road. On the climb back to Whitchurch, Matt decided to go to the front and hammer us all. After a huge effort we got him back, and I said to him, "I don't mind you coming out with us, but don't take the piss by coming out on an ATB bike with training shoes taped to the pedals with gaffer tape!"

"Just wanted to make it hard for myself," he replied.

Matt could always recall how the race went at the weekend. I would get a running commentary of every detail of his races, hence later, he became a brilliant commentator on the top pro races around the world. When he won the British National Road Title he joined Ian Banbury, also a National Road Champion and myself to become life members of the Hemel Hempstead Cycling Club, such a great honour for all three of us.

The Hemel Juniors.

Some of the many juniors that came out of the Hemel Juniors included Tony Clark, who I coached for a while, Nick Walker, Matt Carden, Mark Jervis, Matt Stephens and my son Harvey. All of them put up with some hard, punishing rides through the winter months on the Bob Addy - Hemel training runs, resulting in them winning many races at National level. Most notably the Premier Junior Stage Race in Wales which the club was to dominate. I retain very fond memories of that era.

John Dowling.

Another Hemel rider who shone at racing, was teammate and friend, John Dowling.

An exceptional time trial rider having done a famous sixteen kilometres on his road bike, with no aero equipment and resulting in one of the first riders to go under twenty minutes.

His main forte was as a road man, having ridden in the Tour of Britain and represented Great Britain on several occasions. If not for his job commitments, he would have made a top professional in today's peloton. John was one of the stalwarts of my weekend training runs and even now is a top man to try and beat in events.

Emma Pooley.

The first time I met Emma Pooley was when she was over on one of her many trips to Perth, Western Australia during our summer and the European winter.

I advised her on a technique to improve her time-trialling, bearing in mind that she was already an Olympic silver medallist.

Sometime later, after she had won the World Time Trial Championship in Australia, she rang me to say, "The advice you gave me helped me win that race."

On several occasions Emma came down to my training group where we did a number of extremely hard intervals on which she remarked they were some of the hardest she had ever done. Quite a compliment coming from a rider rated at the time in the top five Women professional riders in the world.

On one occasion Emma arrived late, caught up with us on the training circuit and as we finished and slowed, she said, "I'll carry on and do some more as I arrived late and missed the early ones."

That's what makes a champion.

Alison Dyson.

Alison Dyson is a rider who would have set the world alight if she had been racing in her earlier years. Hard as concrete. A fast learner with a bucket load of determination.

Extremely enthusiastic with many results on the road, track and mountain biking at National and State levels.

Di Otley-Doe.

A very talented rider with similar qualities to Alison Dyson, Di Otley-Doe is a brilliant time trialist who showed how good she was in Great Britain at National level and on the track became the Ladies Military Hour Record holder.

Now living on the east coast of Australia she is giving the ladies a lot of grief over there on the bike.

I've also been honoured to help, train or manage the following:

Paris Roubaix third and fourth.

Tour of Flanders seventh

Great Britain Amateur Road Champion on two occasions.

Great Britain Professional Road Champion three occasions.

Nineteen State Road Champions.

Six Great Britain National Champions.

Many riders representing their countries at the Olympics, Commonwealth Games and World Championships.

World Triathlon Champion.

U.C.I. World Professional Time Trial Champion, one female, one male.

Great Britain Time Trial medallist at sixteen, forty and eighty kilometres.

Sixty-three Club Champions.

And as for myself:

      1967. Holdsworth Team 12 placings in the top ten.
      1968. Holdsworth Team 31 placings in the top ten.
      1969. Holdsworth Team 29 placings in the top ten.
      1970. Holdsworth Team 23 placings in the top ten.
      1971. Holdsworth Team 32 placings in the top ten.
      1972. Ron Kitching Team 32 placings in the top ten.

The National Best All-rounder Competition over eighty, one hundred and sixty kilometres and twelve hours. Placings third, fifth, seventh and tenth.

Professional six-day track rider.

Two years Manager of Team Energy that produced two National Road champions.

Two years National Scottish Team Manager.

Two years Mavic Service Car Tour of Britain.

AUSTRALIA.U.C.I. Fondo Men first, Ladies second place. Thirty-one qualifiers.

Fourteen National Road, criterium and time trial Champions plus numerous podium placings.

Eighteen State Road Champions and again numerous podium placings.

Western Australia State Duathlon Champion.

CHAPTER 31

MY GIRLFRIENDS (Don't tell Wendy)

I have had many girlfriends over the years, but you always hold dear your first one. She was born in Nottingham, United Kingdom.

I first saw her in a magazine, her name was Lenton.

One day, to my utter amazement, she was in a shop.

To my surprise her favourite colours were the same as mine, blue and white, and after many visits I persuaded her to come out with me.

We spent many a happy hour together in the countryside and unbelievably she was to go to the same college. Many a time we would meet afterwards in the bike shed. I was just over 14-years old at the time.

A couple of years later I met another girl, this one from Birmingham, who I could only see at weekends and still naughtily enough, I would see Lenton during the week.

My next girlfriend's name was Paris. One of my friends who'd been with her for a while had spent a fortune taking her to Europe and also purchasing expensive gifts. I mentioned that I fancied her, he said he had had enough of the expensive holidays and I was welcome to take her out.

Well, we hit it off and she became mine.

One of my last girlfriends was an ex-model from France, Miss Peugeot, who I knew for three years before coming to Australia in 2005. Sadly she did not want to come, and I had to leave her behind in Europe.

There have been many more over the years and just recently I have been seeing a very chic Italian girl out in Australia. The only thing is a number of riders in Team Sky have also been going out with her sisters over the last few years as well.

For those that know, you know what I'm talking about!

CHAPTER 32

SUPPORT LETTERS FROM RIDERS ABOUT THE DRILLER

John Dowling

I first encountered Bob as a Junior, although riding in the professional ranks, he stayed in close association with his old club, but for us juniors he was a scary hard man.

As the years went by and my cycling career developed, he was always there to advise and assist, prior to my first Tour of Britain he sent me a good luck card with some tyre savers – a device to flick flints off your tyres before they penetrate – Bob was looking for marginal gains even way back then. All this demonstrates how Bob was a great supporter of the committed, but on the flip side he didn't suffer fools at all which made him unpopular with the less talented or engaged. As time went on, and as Bob's professional career ended, he reverted back to amateur status and we found ourselves racing in the same team. These were great times, we raced hard but had some great experiences.

Although clearly blessed with above average physical talents, Bob's real asset is his ability to ride on the limit and push himself when many others would give in. An expectation he asked of those around him too, which could occasionally be a bit tedious! These comments may paint a picture of a hard-core cycling psychopath but there's a side to Bob not often seen by many; he's a committed husband and family man (although Wendy must be a candidate for sainthood!) and in times of real "non-cycling" need, a great supporter of friends and colleagues. Many have been supported through life's disasters with positivity and perhaps surprising sensitivity.

Bob is very much a 'Marmite man' – you either like him or you don't, and that's fine with him, but nobody can deny that the phrase, "Go hard or go home" could have been invented for him.

Emma Pooley

When I first heard from Bob Addy, while I was in Australia training, I thought he was crazy. After going for a ride with him I knew it for sure! His group sprint sessions were some of the hardest training I've ever done on a bike. Bob is an immensely tough, abrasively gruff, totally uncompromising character who epitomizes the true old school of cycling. His history is incredible, and I'm glad more people will get to hear it.

Matt Stephens

I first met Bob in, I think, 1987 at his bike shop in Watford. My Dad had told me that I needed to join a club and that Bob was a bit of a legend and that this should be my first port of call. So I went to Bob Addy Cycles in Watford as a young 17-year-old. I walked to the counter, saw a tall, drawn, but fit looking older chap and asked, "Are you Bob Addy?"

"Yes," the slightly scary looking man replied.

"I'd like to join a cycling club," I said, rather nervously.

Bob then said nothing, but simply reached for a pamphlet on the counter, housed in Perspex, which he gave to me. I looked at the simple, folded piece of A4 paper which was headlined, 'Hemel Hempstead CC.'

"What do I do?" I asked the frightening looking man. I was actually quite scared at this point.

"Turn up on Thursday. We have a club night."

"Ok," I replied. Then popped the pamphlet in my pocket and got out of the shop as fast as I could.

The next Thursday I rode my bike to the club room in Kings Langley where my future as a cyclist was forged. The 'Hemel' would be my cycling home from that point onwards with Bob a central part of it.

Looking back, I can honestly say that those days, in the mid to late 80's when on club runs with the Hemel and Bob, were some of the most enjoyable of my life. It was certainly a school of hard knocks with Bob, who never gave a quarter when riding on the front. They were fun days, but hard days. Bob was a hard guy to like as he always made us suffer, but this was a skill I took and honed myself. I learnt so much from Bob, but mostly about the cruel beauty of cycling.

Thanks Bob. You helped give me an edge. A side to me I didn't like, but a side to me that helped me win.

CHAPTER 33

WHY DID THEY CALL ME 'THE DRILLER'?

It's been mentioned a few times in here about my training regimes, so I thought I would leave you with an insight into the methods I used and those that I subsequently passed on to others. I found them hard, it wasn't that I breezed through them, but you get used to it and yes, I would drill it into those who rode with me in a way that perhaps made me come across as hard on them. The truth is, I was. If you want to win, you have to be disciplined, you have to put in the effort and you have to work. There is no apology given by me on that score.

Regarding a typical week of training. The first thing to say is there is no one routine that you can stick to all year, or even all season. In the majority of weeks the training would be different depending on the time of year and also the forth coming target events, but as best as I can 'summarise', this would be the run down for some of the weeks.

Early in the year, and when I was a young rider (so about two minutes ago in my head and over 65 years ago in reality) I'd do gym work on four mornings and two evenings a week. Plus two evenings of weights only. This was supplemented by 800 kms on the bike and factor in that if you aren't a professional yet, you'll be doing this as I was, whilst working a full-time job between 9 – 5.30pm, five days a week. Also if you are in the Northern Hemisphere, you'll be doing this in the cold of late winter and early spring, from January to March. If you are down in the Southern Hemisphere you have the heat and flies to contend with.

Back up in the UK where I was doing most of my riding as a young man, gym work would gradually taper down as the year progressed and the evenings became lighter, giving way to racing midweek and weekends.

All seems okay so far. Well it was, but my Dad was the driver to my training and he had his own methods to push me. At some of the races, if I didn't perform very well, (not finishing in the top six) and the event was being held within 100 kms of home, my Dad would say, "You better ride home." This would be after a race of 120 to 160 kms.

Midweek races, track and road would be treated as training races for the weekend which entailed racing very aggressively and attacking the field at every opportunity. Looking back it was a crude, but effective, form of interval training.

How do I know it was effective? Many of my rivals would comment, I can beat you during the week but at weekend races or a big event, you are always up in the prizes.

If there was no racing in the midweek, especially in the heart of the season, I'd stick to the following schedule:

- Monday: Two hours recovery ride.
- Tuesday evening: Chain gang (12/15 riders going at in many cases above race speed for a distance of between 80 to 100 kms).
- Wednesday: 3 hours steady.
- Thursday evening: Chain gang.
- Friday: Two hours easy.
- As well as on most mornings a ride of at least one and a half hours during the week.
- Saturday and Sunday: Races.

When we owned the shop and I had commercial and business responsibilities I would amend it to be:

- Monday: Two hours easy.
- Tuesday: Three and a half hours very early medium pace. In the evening one hour 15 minutes flat out.
- Wednesday: One hour 15 minutes in morning and one hour 15 minutes flat out in the evening.
- Thursday: Same as Tuesday, so nearly five hours in total.
- Friday: One hour each way.
- Saturday: Car in, no bike.
- Sunday: Race.

In Australia, I was retired, so things got a lot more relaxed. Well, sort of.

- Monday: Easy two hours.
- Tuesday: 100 kms - after an easy ride of 20 kms to North Dandulup would be race speed for another 80kms to Dwellingup, after the descent towards Pinjarra on the flat, a group of 4 to 6 riders would keep the speed at 50 km an hour plus for 15 kms.
- Wednesday: Could be interval sprints 3 per lap x 3 = 9. One lap easy and repeat twice more for a total of 27 sprints.
- Thursday: Dwellingup, (about 100kms out from Perth).
- Friday: Rest day.
- Saturday: Easy two hours or race.
- Sunday: Race.

But as I said, if I was planning for a target event, like Classics, Tours, State and National titles, then training would be different depending on the distances, locations etc.

All in all, you need to put the kilometres in. You need to keep the pace up and if it isn't feeling painful, it probably isn't doing you much good. Remember what Eddy Merckx said, "Cyclists live with pain. If you can't handle it you will win nothing."

So grit your teeth, dig in and go faster, harder, longer. Sprint harder and faster, do more of them. Keep your body tough and do it tough. Yes, look after your diet and yes, get as much sleep as you can. And for reasons that I believe in but others may not, elevate your legs while asleep. And if you do all of that will you win and be a Champion? No, of course not.

To do that, you need belief, a cast-iron will, an unerring desire and bags of determination. You'll need good people around you, great team mates at your back, supportive partners by your side and friends who will cajole and belittle and boost you in the way only friends can. Ultimately, even with all of that, you'll also need a massive side serve of luck; for punctures and crashes and the Cycling God of 'Shit-Happens' isn't going to be bought off by all the training in the world. But I can guarantee you one thing. Without the hard training, all the rest will count for naught.

Yet, at the end of the day, none of that matters if you aren't having fun at some point. Yeah, you'll swear and curse at the freezing early mornings, you'll wonder what the heck you are doing out on a lonely road in the middle of the evening when others you know are tucked up in front of their TV with a glass or two of wine or beer. You will swear and weep and bleed and hurt but deep down, when you are travelling at 50 or 60 kms per hour on two wheels barely wider than your finger, you will love it. You have to love cycling to be a cyclist. It was and is my life, my life cycle if you will, and so I'd be insane to have done it for this long and not love it.

Just don't tell anyone I said that last bit. I mean, I can hardly be the hardest of 'Drillers' if I have that soft side, now can I?

Anyway, I hope this has given you some insight into a little of the training that I did. I wish you open roads and happy days.

Bob Addy OLY

Mandurah, Western Australia

2022

Acknowledgements

To Brian Buck for pushing me into writing this and to Australian Commonwealth Games double silver medallist, Murray Hall, who has assisted me with the editing, and guidance through the processes of bringing my story to publication. But mostly to Wendy. For being there. Always.

About the Author

Robert Addy (Bob) was born in Luton, United Kingdom, in 1941. Initially training as a draughtsman he went on to pursue his love of cycling, becoming British National Road Champion after turning professional and representing Great Britain in well over 100 races in many of the cycling world's most prestigious events, including racing the 55th Tour de France. Later becoming a cycling shop owner, business man, cycling coach and cycling team manager, Bob Addy's life has never ventured far from two wheels.

Now, even in his 80s, Bob rides daily and his continuing fitness is testament to the man whose training regimes were so hard and tough that he was known as 'The Driller'.

CPSIA information can be obtained
at www.ICGtesting.com
Printed in the USA
LVHW070426271022
731428LV00006B/6